The Historian's Narrative of Frederick Douglass

Recent Titles in The Historian's Annotated Classics Series

The Historian's Huck Finn: Reading Mark Twain's Masterpiece as Social and Economic History
Annotated by Ranjit S. Dighe

The Historian's Narrative of Frederick Douglass

Reading Douglass's Autobiography as Social and Cultural History

☙❧

Edited by
Robert Felgar

The Historian's Annotated Classics
Ranjit S. Dighe, Series Editor

PRAEGER™

An Imprint of ABC-CLIO, LLC
Santa Barbara, California • Denver, Colorado

Text of Douglass's *Narrative* courtesy of Documenting the American South, Wilson Special Collections Library, UNC-Chapel Hill.

Library of Congress Cataloging-in-Publication Data

Names: Felgar, Robert. Historian's narrative of Frederick Douglass. | Douglass, Frederick, 1818–1895. Narrative of the life of Frederick Douglass, an American slave.
Title: The historian's narrative of Frederick Douglass : reading Douglass's autobiography as social and cultural history / edited by Robert Felgar.
Description: Santa Barbara, California : Praeger, an Imprint of ABC-CLIO, LLC, 2017. | Series: The historian's annotated classics | Includes bibliographical references and index.
Identifiers: LCCN 2017013770 | ISBN 9781440846861 (hardback) | ISBN 9781440843099 (paperback) | ISBN 9781440843105 (Ebook)
Subjects: LCSH: Douglass, Frederick, 1818-1895. Narrative of the life of Frederick Douglass, an American slave. | Slaves' writings, American—Study and teaching. | African American abolitionists—Biography. | Slaves—United States—Biography. | Slavery—United States—History—Study and teaching.
Classification: LCC E449.D75 H57 2017 | DDC 973.7114092 [B] —dc23 LC record available at https://lccn.loc.gov/2017013770

ISBN: 978-1-4408-4686-1 (hardcover)
       978-1-4408-4309-9 (pbk.)
EISBN: 978-1-4408-4310-5

21 20 19 18 17   1 2 3 4 5

This book is also available as an eBook.

Praeger
An Imprint of ABC-CLIO, LLC

ABC-CLIO, LLC
130 Cremona Drive, P.O. Box 1911
Santa Barbara, California 93116-1911
www.abc-clio.com

This book is printed on acid-free paper ∞
Manufactured in the United States of America

To Cindy

ञ८०

Contents

Series Foreword

Most if not all literature is historical, in the sense of reflecting its time and place and the history behind them. Even science fiction and fantasy literature tends to extrapolate from the present, which, like a patient, has a history of its own. Works from previous eras take on an additional historical dimension, as they were written in a time with which we are personally unfamiliar.

While great works of literature are timeless, we can often enjoy them more by knowing more about their historical setting and the by-now-obscure references they sometimes make. This is where Praeger's Historian's Annotated Classics series comes in. The literary classics selected for this series are accompanied by annotations and new essays that highlight their historical context and continuing relevance.

Ultimately, this series is about connecting each book to crucial historical issues of its time. Novels, biographies, and other literature of a time are indispensable markers of what people of that time said and thought. Thus this series should be ideal for people with a strong interest in history—students, history teachers, history buffs. The books in this series can also be valuable supplementary texts that add spice to college and advanced high school classes. Being able to see history through the lens of an enduring work from that era makes the material considerably more vivid.

The Historian's Annotated Narrative of the Life of Frederick Douglass arrives at nearly the same time as the bicentennial celebration of Douglass's birth. Douglass was perhaps the most famous and eloquent abolitionist, and his autobiography is one of the most searing and vivid depictions of slavery ever written. Douglass's unadorned but powerful prose remains accessible almost two centuries later. For an introduction to the horror that was American slavery, one could hardly do better than Douglass's first-hand account. Douglass's gripping narrative, which ends with his escape from slavery at about age twenty, will likely leave readers wanting to know more about Douglass's long and extraordinary life and about slavery itself. Felgar's annotations and essays provide exactly that.

The annotations offer helpful details on aspects of slavery that Douglass mentions and explain some obscure references. In addition, we learn about Douglass's alliances with William Lloyd Garrison, John Brown, and Abraham Lincoln; Douglass's evolving views on the tactics of freeing the slaves; and what Emancipation meant to Douglass and other African Americans.

Ranjit S. Dighe
Professor of Economics
State University of New York at Oswego

ය‍ශ‍ව

Preface

I admire *Narrative of the Life of Frederick Douglass* because it is such a compelling and powerful story of overcoming a system designed to crush slaves. Douglass refused to accept the preposterous notion that he and his fellow blacks were inferior to whites in any way. He knew that internalizing a lie would help perpetuate a social institution that had to be destroyed, and as he came to understand, by civil war if necessary. He and white abolitionists realized that his autobiography could serve as a key piece of written evidence of the depth of slavery's evil and of what it felt like to be a slave. This is what slavery is like, Douglass's story proclaims, and how much longer is it going to last, is what his story is asking.

I admire it, too, because the author is so skillful at creating a version of himself that will appeal to his readers and gain their support for his cause. The Douglass we engage with is uncommonly intelligent, a polished stylist, a person with an incredible memory and a robust ego, a man of physical courage, a man who valued friendship very highly, and a man with the will and determination to escape slavery, in other words, a man we respect highly and wish to emulate.

The tale of Douglass's early life is admirable also for its high literary quality: the polished sentences, products of carefully chosen diction and elegant syntax, show his skill and pleasure in writing. And his numerous references, allusions, and quotations enrich his resonant life story. Particularly of note are Douglass's metaphors, the gash in his foot that could accommodate the quill pen he writes with and Colonel Lloyd's garden being unforgettable examples. The powerful scenes of dialogue, especially between Douglass and the slavebreaker Covey, dramatize the young Douglass's desperate situation effectively, however much Douglass relied on was his imagination rather than the actual words that were spoken. The overall sweep of the narrative, from the author's childhood to his escape from slavery, is moving and exciting: Douglass knew how to use his literary skills to help change the course of American history.

I wrote this book to bring home to the contemporary reader that Douglass is one of the most fascinating people who ever lived. His remarkable sensibility missed little: he was interested in practically everything, from the spirituals to literacy, to economics, to politics, to, especially, people. Unusually perceptive, he saw through the hypocrisy of white religious and moral pretensions to good literary effect in his autobiography. He possessed a rare determination, self-confidence, and willpower that stood him well in his defeat of slavery and rise to prominence in the battle to destroy it. His spectacular oratorical power meant he would be the most capable public speaker in nineteenth-century America.

Also among this book's goals is making *Narrative of the Life of Frederick Douglass* accessible to the contemporary reader. Because it is so densely allusive, many of today's readers will be adrift without readily available explanations and identifications of Douglass's numerous references to and quotations from the Bible, and references to secular literature, nineteenth-century United States politics and history. Even the most capable users of smart phones and other electronic devices are liable to be daunted by Douglass's text, unless the necessary scholarly apparatus is readily available, as it is in this edition. My chapters on Douglass's life and times provide what today's readers need in the way of contextualization. Readers will have within one volume what they need to enjoy and comprehend what is still *the* slave narrative in many readers' judgment.

My third purpose in writing this book is to demonstrate that Douglass represents a major step forward in a process that may well be a permanent part of United States history: that everyone is human, regardless of how they look, speak, dress, and live; if this is so, then why are some people treated as if they are less than human? Douglass had a keen sense of the innate dignity and worth of everyone, in large measure because of what he observed in his own case: a capable man being treated as an "inferior" by people whose skin was lighter than his.

I believe this book can be a major aid to classroom teachers. The annotations provide a wealth of information and ideas that make the text comprehensible and enjoyable. Because the annotations are embedded in the text, teachers will not have to spend their limited time flipping back and forth to endnotes. The annotations can be used as springboards to further reading, discussion, research, and paper topics, such as the crucial importance of literacy. The introductory chapters contain the essential background information about Douglass's life and times that students and their teachers need for his autobiography. The emphasis in the chapters and annotations is on what will be directly useful information and concepts for today's teachers and their students.

෬෮

Acknowledgments

Many thanks once again to Susan Hurst, English Department Secretary at Jacksonville State University, for her excellent typing and general good will. And also to Michael Millman, acquisitions editor at Praeger, and Ranjit Dighe, series editor of the Historian's Annotated Classics series, the former for his strong support and encouragement, and the latter for his uncommonly astute editorial work.

ରେ୫ଠ

Chronology

Date	Key Events in American History	Key Events in Frederick Douglass's Life
1776	Declaration of Independence ("all [white] men are created equal").	
1781	The thirteen colonies form a confederation.	
1788	U.S. Constitution ratified (is it pro- or antislavery?).	
1793	Invention of cotton gin by Eli Whitney makes slavery extremely profitable.	
1807	International slave trade officially abolished but not the internal slave trade.	
1818		Frederick Douglass born in Talbot County, Maryland (though he died not knowing the year of his birth or who his father was).
1820	The Missouri Compromise allows Missouri to enter the United States as a slave state.	

Date	Key Events in American History	Key Events in Frederick Douglass's Life
1824		Douglass's grandmother takes him to the Wye House plantation.
1826–1827		Douglass is sent to live with the Auld family in Baltimore, where Sophia Auld teaches him the alphabet.
1831	William Lloyd Garrison establishes *The Liberator*, the foremost abolitionist newspaper.	
1833		Douglass violently resists the slavebreaker Edward Covey's attempts to control him, an episode of the utmost importance in Douglass's experiences.
1836		Douglass's first attempt to escape from slavery is unsuccessful.
1838		His second attempt succeeds, as he and his soon-to-be first wife, Anna Murray, make it safely to New Bedford, Massachusetts.
1839		Douglass's first daughter, Rosetta, is born.
1840		Birth of Douglass's first son, Lewis Henry Douglass.
1841		Douglass, at Garrison's urging, speaks to the Massachusetts Anti-Slavery Society convention.
1842		Birth of Frederick Douglass Jr.
1844		Third son, Charles Remond Douglass, born.

Date	Key Events in American History	Key Events in Frederick Douglass's Life
1845		Douglass publishes the first of three versions of his autobiography *Narrative of the Life of Frederick Douglass, An American Slave.*
1845–1846		Douglass delivers numerous antislavery speeches throughout the British Isles.
1848		Douglass and Garrison begin to distance themselves from each other.
1849		Last child, Annie, born (dies in 1860).
1850	The Fugitive Slave Act passed by Congress; it is more severe than a previous one.	
1851		Douglass merges the *North Star* with the white abolitionist Gerrit Smith's paper to form *Frederick Douglass' Paper.*
1852	Publication of Harriet Beecher Stowe's *Uncle Tom's Cabin*, a phenomenal best seller that attacked slavery.	Douglass delivers one of his most famous speeches, "What to the Slave is the Fourth of July?" in Rochester, New York, on July 5, 1852.
1853		Douglass publishes his only known work of prose fiction, *The Heroic Slave*, based on a successful slave revolt aboard the *Creole* in 1841.
1855		Douglass publishes the second version of his life's story, *My Bondage and My Freedom*, in which he is more candid about Garrison than he could be in the 1845 version.

Date	Key Events in American History	Key Events in Frederick Douglass's Life
1857	The Dred Scott decision: the Supreme Court, under Judge Taney, rules that Congress cannot abolish slavery in the states, and African Americans have no rights that a white man needs to respect.	
1859	John Brown's Raid, an unsuccessful attempt to gain control of the Federal arsenal at Harpers Ferry.	Douglass refuses to accept Brown's invitation to join the raid.
1860	Abraham Lincoln is elected president, which means the end of slavery.	
1861	The Civil War begins; it will end four years later.	
1863	The Emancipation Proclamation declares the slaves in the Confederate states are free (not in the northern border states).	Douglass recruits African American men for the Union Army (his sons Lewis and Charles will fight for the Union). Douglass publishes "Why Should a Colored Man Enlist."
1865	The Civil War ends with the defeat of Confederate troops. President Lincoln is assassinated. The 13th Amendment to the Constitution (prohibition of slavery) is ratified. Reconstruction begins (and ends in 1877).	
1866	Black Codes put into effect in former states of the Confederacy.	
1868	Ratification of 14th Amendment, which nullifies the Dred Scott decision.	

Date	Key Events in American History	Key Events in Frederick Douglass's Life
1870	Ratification of 15th Amendment, which grants black Americans the right to vote.	
1872		Douglass delivers one of his most popular speeches, "Self-Made Men," and many times thereafter.
1874		Douglass becomes President of the Freedmen's Bank, which goes under.
1876		Douglass delivers one of his most important speeches at the unveiling of the Freedmen's Monument, in Lincoln Park, Washington, D.C.
1877	End of Reconstruction: the withdrawal of federal troops from the former Confederacy means the civil rights of black southerners will be negligible at best.	Douglass is appointed U.S. Marshall of the District of Columbia.
1878		Douglass buys Cedar Hill House, giving him an excellent view of Washington, D.C.
1879	Many blacks begin leaving the South in hopes of a better life in the North.	
1881	First Jim Crow laws passed in Tennessee, and eventually the rest of the South, to segregate black people from whites on trains.	Douglass publishes the third version of his life's story, *Life and Times of Frederick Douglass.*
1882		Anna Murray Douglass dies.
1884		Douglass marries his second wife, Helen Pitts.

Date	Key Events in American History	Key Events in Frederick Douglass's Life
1889		Douglass appointed Chargé d'Affairs, Santo Domingo. Douglass appointed U.S. Minister Resident and Consul General to Haiti. Many were perplexed by his support of the annexation of Santo Domingo.
1892		Expanded version of *Life and Times of Frederick Douglass* appears.
1893		Douglass delivers speech at the World's Fair in Chicago. Black Americans were almost completely excluded from this fair.
1895		Douglass dies of heart failure after giving a speech on women's rights.
1896		The Supreme Court rules racial segregation is legal.

CHAPTER 1

ೞೞೞ

Frederick Douglass:
Slave and Free

As the scholarship on Frederick Douglass continues to grow, it is becoming increasingly clear that he was one of the most remarkable people who ever lived. Born a slave in 1818, in the state of Maryland, he triumphed over slavery to become a giant in nineteenth-century American history whose only real rival for preeminence was Abraham Lincoln, another self-made man. Not only was Douglass the most important abolitionist in American history, he was also a key figure in American literature, and remains so today. He became a foreign diplomat, a friend of Lincoln, a major journalist, a spectacular orator, a multimillionaire (in today's dollars), a husband, a father, a doting grandfather, a neighborhood figure beloved by children, a violinist, a world traveler, and much more. A man who did not even know the exact date of his birth—just one of slavery's strategies to deny him any sense of being a human being—grew up to become uncommonly intelligent, extremely influential, admired by untold numbers of black and white Americans, and a shaper of American destiny.

How he managed to do all this is amazing but comprehensible, because Douglass had an uncanny ability to take advantage of every opportunity and willpower strong beyond measure, as well as an insatiable intellectual curiosity. What makes his rise even more impressive is that he was never told who his father, a white man, was, and barely knew his mother, a black woman who had a very strong character, named Harriet Bailey. His father may have been Aaron Anthony, his first master, but this has yet to be accepted as fact. In other words, Douglass began life in circumstances that would have foreclosed any chance for a life of extraordinary accomplishments for most people. He was born in the country of Maryland's Eastern Shore and saw his mother to know her as his mother only a few times when he was little; she died when he was about seven, an event that meant almost nothing to a son who by then regarded her as a stranger. He was not allowed to attend her funeral.

These slaves are dressed in typical clothing and using tools and equipment found on many plantations. (Library of Congress)

His childhood was not utterly bleak, though. He was given some freedom—freedom in a highly limited sense—to play with other slave children on the spectacular Lloyd Plantation on the Eastern Shore in Maryland, an area he retained nostalgic affection for, even as an adult (it was slavery Douglass despised, not where he experienced it). His incredible memory recalled many accurate details of his childhood on this plantation, including the disturbing experience of watching his Aunt Hester stripped to the waist and whipped: seeing this horrifying incident traumatized Douglass as a child, especially because he had never seen anything like it before and expected to be next.

In 1826 he was sent to Baltimore to work for Sophia and Hugh Auld. Partly through Sophia's help, and partly through his own efforts, he learned to read and write, which led to his profound and lasting transformation: he came to understand that literacy was the key to unlock the mystery of how whites had the upper hand over blacks. A literate black person is a threat to slavery and white racism, the young Douglass began to understand, because in a print-based culture, literacy brings knowledge of the texts, such as the Bible and the Constitution, over which white readers had control in the white South. Black literacy meant an end to white control of the interpretation of key writings that had been used to justify slavery, such as the story of Ham in Genesis, whose descendants were supposedly cursed to be slaves because Ham saw his father naked.

This would be like the Lloyd Plantation, where Douglass spent much of his boyhood. (Library of Congress)

Seven years later, in 1833, Douglass was sent back to the Lloyd Plantation in Maryland. Because he did not get along with his owner, Thomas Auld (Hugh Auld's brother), he was sent to live with a slavebreaker named Edward Covey. Covey deliberately ordered Douglass to accompany a pair of oxen that was hitched to a wagon into the woods, knowing the young slave knew nothing of handling oxen. Inevitably, the wagon was damaged when it crashed into a tree: this was the chance Covey used to confront Douglass, which led to a fight that, as Douglass reports and represents it, he won. This fight is one of the most important incidents in African American history and literature, because regardless of the numerous disagreements over it, it remains a powerful argument in favor of the necessity of violence in some situations if black people are going to be treated with respect in their own country. Whether it actually happened as Douglass reported it in the *Narrative* or the way he reported it in *My Bondage and My Freedom* ten years later in 1855 is not as significant as the fact that self-defense is crucial to the destruction of "the peculiar institution," as slavery was described in the twisted language of the Old South. Standing up to Covey made Douglass feel like a man, and black manhood is what, in key ways, nineteenth-century African

Douglass may well have seen a group of slaves chained together like this. Madison Washington, the hero of Douglass's *The Heroic Slave*, definitely did. (Library of Congress)

American history is about. Eventually, Douglass came to realize that violence on a massive scale would be the only way the masters could be forced to give up legal slavery.

A few years later, in 1836, Douglass returned to Baltimore to learn how to seal the seams in ships, that is, to master the calking trade. Little did he know that some of these ships were destined for work in the slave trade. As a calker, he became more literate because letters of the alphabet were used to indicate where a particular piece of wood was to go. He also fought again, this time against a gang of white laborers who resented competition with a black man for work. And again, he handled himself well, even though this time he faced more than one white opponent and was wounded in one eye.

While working in Baltimore's shipyards, Douglass also met the woman who would become his first wife, a free black woman named Anna Murray; although she was virtually illiterate, she was extremely skilled at managing their household affairs after they were married and had children. Her daughter Rosetta remembered her especially fondly. Douglass was able to save money from his work as a calker to use in his planned escape to the North, a plan Anna also helped him with (an earlier attempt to flee had failed because one of Douglass's fellow slaves, later named by Douglass as Sandy Jenkins, betrayed Douglass

Douglass's African ancestors would have crossed the Atlantic on a ship like this one. (Library of Congress)

and several close companions). In other words, the rugged individualism many of Douglass's admirers recognize in him, was complicated by crucial active help from his first wife. He was also fortunate that a man Douglass thought recognized him when he disguised himself as a merchant sailor during his second and successful attempt to escape from slavery kept his mouth shut.

Douglass was struck by the fact that in many ways he had gone up South rather than up North when he arrived safely in New York City on September 4, 1838. He quickly realized that although he was a fugitive slave instead of a slave, he was not regarded by northern whites as their social equal; particularly galling was the condescension he experienced even at the hands of white abolitionists, such as the most famous one, William Lloyd Garrison. True freedom for Douglass and millions of his fellow black Americans since then remained and has remained elusive. Douglass was "free" in the North, not free.

He was naturally intensely interested in the antislavery societies in the North, and when Garrison asked Douglass to speak at a rally the latter was attending, Douglass nervously accepted. This is how Douglass's career as a public speaker began, a career that continued into the last year of his life, 1895. In the nineteenth century in America, a

Always extremely conscious of his appearance, the young Douglass knew this likeness would convince society that he was a gentleman. (Library of Congress)

man standing six feet tall and weighing two hundred pounds was an imposing figure. Douglass was also well proportioned, muscular, and handsome, as well as gifted with a sonorous voice and a commanding presence. He possessed as well wit, logic, and charisma: all these virtues resulted in the most brilliant orator in a century of United States history remembered for its orators, such as Garrison, Daniel Webster, and Henry Clay. It should be noted, though, that William T. Wilson, writing under the name "Ethiop," in "A Leaf from My Scrap Book: Samuel R. [Ringgold] Ward and Frederick Douglass," published in *Autographs for Freedom*, edited by Julia Griffiths (1854), says Douglass sometimes substituted words for ideas when giving a speech, whereas Ward always uses ideas as the basis of his oratory. Douglass's most notable speeches include "What to the Slave Is the Fourth of July?," "The Self-Made Man," and his address delivered at the unveiling of the Freedmen's Monument in Lincoln Park, Washington, D.C. While under Garrison's influence, Douglass's abolitionist speeches had to stick to the Garrison party line: moral suasion was the answer to ending slavery. After Douglass and his mentor went separate ways, the former came to realize that there was only one way to end slavery, and that was war.

Douglass became so impressive and successful as a public speaker that doubts over whether or not he had actually been a slave began to circulate. To contradict them and to create a literary as well as an actual image of himself, he wrote the first of three versions of his autobiography, *Narrative of the Life of Frederick Douglass, An American Slave, Written by Himself*, published in 1845. The second phrase of the title, *An American Slave*, is at the heart of the author's life, as well as of

American history: how can a country that is supposedly based on freedom be based also on slavery? It is this unreconcilable contradiction that Douglass spent his life trying to destroy. The book was a bestseller, having sold over 30,000 copies by 1850; it remains *the* slave narrative in many scholars' estimation, although his second version of his life's story, *My Bondage and My Freedom* (1855), is getting increasing attention, partly because Douglass could be much more candid about white abolitionists such as Garrison and Wendell Phillips than he could be when they provided a preface and an introductory letter to the first version of his autobiography. They wanted Douglass to be their representative specimen of what a slave should be like, not an autonomous agent.

Even though he and Douglass had a permanent falling out, Douglass praised Garrison, the most famous abolitionist in the nineteenth century, when he died. (Library of Congress)

Douglass was justifiably so concerned about being recaptured and returned to slavery that from 1845 to 1847 he went to the British Isles to deliver numerous speeches on abolition. He was well received there, although on the voyage across the Atlantic on the *Cambria*, a mob of proslavery white American passengers demanded that Douglass be kept to his cabin; fortunately, the captain supported Douglass. In the British Isles Douglass particularly treasured being viewed as a social equal, an experience that confirmed his opinion that racism was learned behavior and thus could be unlearned. He never lost faith that education was the way to destroy racial prejudice in the United States.

Upon his return, he decided to start his own abolitionist newspaper, *The North Star*, named after the star that fugitive slaves followed on their way north. Garrison did not at all accept the idea of a paper edited and largely written by a black man that would compete with his own *Liberator*. Garrison's feelings were also hurt by what he viewed as his protégé's rejection of Garrison in the role of a father figure. By the early 1850s, Douglass had changed his mind about the Constitution being a proslavery document, whereas Garrison maintained it was; Douglass also came to realize that moral persuasion was not going to end slavery and that violence would be necessary. Garrison could not abide disagreement with his policies, let alone his former pupil making his own decisions without consulting him. Eventually, the relationship between Garrison and Douglass degenerated into Garrison, without proof, accusing Douglass of having an affair with the editor of *Autographs for Freedom*; she lived with the Douglasses while she helped with his newspaper work. Anna Murray Douglass supposedly wrote a letter contradicting Garrison, but its authenticity has been challenged because of her illiteracy. Still, when his former mentor died in 1879, Douglass wrote very warmly of him, saying he was a decent man.

After *The North Star* merged with Gerrit Smith's *Liberty Party Paper* in 1851 to become *Frederick Douglass' Paper* (Smith was a wealthy white abolitionist and one of John Brown's supporters in the raid on Harpers Ferry), Douglass published his short novel *The Heroic Slave* (1853) in it. His only published work of prose fiction, it is recognized now as a remarkable portrait of an actual figure, Madison Washington, who led a slave revolt upon the slave ship *Creole* in 1839. Clearly, Douglass greatly admired Madison Washington and tried to seek him out in Haiti, where he settled after the revolt, but was unsuccessful. In Madison Washington, Douglass saw the black hero he himself probably wanted to be. He is careful to emphasize in *The Heroic Slave* that Washington uses violence only to the degree it is necessary: when Washington's followers on the *Creole* want revenge on a member of the white crew after their successful revolt, Washington forbids it. Douglass is walking a tightrope between *Uncle Tom's Cabin*, published in 1852 and representing Uncle Tom as a saintly figure who would never advocate or use violence to end slavery, and Herman Melville's *Benito Cereno*, published in 1855, in which the leader of the slave revolt on the *San Dominick*, Babo, is cunning in his use of violence not only to overthrow the Spanish crew but also to terrorize the survivors, particularly Benito Cereno, the Spanish captain whose throat Babo threatens to slit as he shaves him. *Uncle Tom's Cabin* was being debated in *Frederick Douglass' Paper* while *The Heroic Slave* was being published in it. Douglass appears to be trying to support the restrained use of violence in the service of the abolition of slavery. Consequently, part of Douglass's triumph over slavery is that he rejected its frequent reliance on sadistic violence to maintain itself in favor of a necessary use of violence to end slavery.

The Heroic Slave is not only a powerful recreation of the most successful slave insurrection in United States history, it is also a pointed defense of black violence to overthrow slavery. Madison Washington notes that if he and his fellow African rebels are murderers (two members of the white crew on the *Creole* are killed), then so were the white patriots of 1776. Douglass's depictions of the state of Virginia in Part I and of the public tavern in Part II of *The Heroic Slave* indicate that he believed the abolition of slavery would reinvigorate not only the lives of slaves but also the early promise of the Declaration of Independence, which had fallen on hard times in the eyes of the former slave and his abolitionist allies. The revolt on board the *Creole*, in other words, signified to Douglass a prelude to a civil war that would bring about a new birth of freedom.

Two years after the appearance of *The Heroic Slave*, Douglass published the second version of his autobiography, *My Bondage and My Freedom* (1855). He felt comfortable being more candid in 1855 than in 1845 because he was no longer under the sway of the Garrisonians. By choosing a black man, Dr. James McCune Smith, to write the introduction, Douglass did not have to tolerate the patronizing attitudes of Garrison and Wendell Phillips, who provided the introductory matter for *Narrative of the Life of Frederick Douglass*, published ten years earlier. As the first black medical doctor (although he was not allowed to join the American Medical Association), Smith fully recognized and respected Douglass's victory over slavery. Pointing out that while Douglass justified the goals of the United States antislavery movement by becoming free and successful, Smith acknowledged that in the North Douglass faced the daunting task of overcoming caste-slavery, that is, social prejudice based on skin color. Wendell Phillips and William Lloyd Garrison failed to understand that Douglass was already at least their equal, not just in potential but in actual eloquence and reasoning. Had they, and other northern whites, been capable of acknowledging Douglass's achievements and potential, they would have also had to admit that being white was not an achievement worth note, a truth that probably no white American in the nineteenth century could have recognized. Smith made the insightful point, too, that Douglass's work as a newspaper editor was compelling evidence of the practicality and wisdom of Immediate Emancipation (in contrast to the gradualism favored by many white abolitionists). So much black potential was wasted because slaves had not been given the opportunity to realize their potential. As the nineteenth century progressed, Smith and innumerable other observers, rightfully indicated Douglass as the irrefutable counterevidence to the assumption that slaves were inferior to whites, suggesting that the reason some whites were opposed to abolition is their fear that African Americans were not only not their inferiors, but if given the same opportunities whites had, their superiors.

In the 1850s Douglass also devoted much of his time and energy to attacking the Fugitive Slave Act, a notorious law that required the return of runaway slaves to their owners; violating it could result in fines and imprisonment, while supporting it resulted in financial rewards. The act brought home to white northerners that slavery had a far greater significance for them after its passage than they realized, when they were directly confronted with its effects. Many of its denouncers did not realize in 1850 that a law designed to lessen tensions between the South and the North ended up increasing them to the point that a civil war broke out in 1861 between the two sections of the country: a piece of legislation its supporters thought would preserve slavery was one of the reasons legal slavery collapsed, although it survived in the form of a racial prejudice that is far from abolished a century and a half after the Civil War ended in 1865.

In the 1850s Douglass also further exposed slavery and racism's weaknesses in a poem and several speeches. The poem, "The Tyrants' Jubilee!" (1857), reveals his bitter but mischievous sense of humor in an attack on the masters of the Old South (the tyrants of the title), who worry that the slave insurrections in the 1850s portended a more apocalyptic clash that would overwhelm the whole system of slavery, which of course is what began to happen in 1861. The speaker is imagined to be a slaveholder who is appalled that some slaves are not grateful for what whites have provided them in the way of food, clothing, shelter, and enlightenment. Douglass depicts him as a combination of complacency and fear about what could happen, but did not. Douglass lived to expose the moral hollowness of the masters in their total blindness to what they were doing to black people. It is obvious now, and was becoming increasingly clearer to Douglass in 1857, that cataclysmic violence was the only solution to the overwhelming evil of slavery. Celebrating a jubilee at a historical pause in the fight against slavery indicates the hopelessness of relying on the Garrisonian emphasis on persuasion to abolish slavery.

Douglass's most famous speech, "What to the Slave is the Fourth of July?," delivered ironically on July 5, 1852, is another example of his building a stronger and stronger case against slavery. He began by pointing out that July 4 is not the birthday of the national independence of black people but of whites; however, since the nation was only seventy-six years old, there is hope for the abolitionists because seventy-six is a young age for a nation; it may be able to change its course, whereas an older one might be too set in its traditions to change. He then implied that the fathers of his listeners were to the English government in 1776 what the slaves are to the federal government in 1852: just as the patriots in 1776 wanted their freedom and independence, so did African Americans want theirs in 1852. To put his point another way, Douglas asked his audience what he and his fellow African Americans have to do with a day celebrating national independence: the answer of course is nothing. The fourth was a day of overwhelming sadness to black people because it and what it stands for, freedom, have no connection to slaves. Quoting his former mentor, William Lloyd Garrison, Douglas proclaimed he too will not equivocate or excuse American slavery.

In response to the charges that abolitionists should argue more and attack less, Douglass asked what there is to argue about, in particular regarding whether or not black men are men or not. But then he shrewdly went ahead and argued anyway, knowing that what is self-evident is not always accepted as so. Consequently, he observed that black men can do whatever white men can do, including reading, writing, cyphering, and engaging in the same jobs whites perform. His most telling blow was delivered when he declared that every man knows slavery is wrong for him. This is a time, Douglass proclaimed, not for arguing, but for thunder, storm, whirlwind, and earthquake—in other words, a time for the violent abolition of slavery.

After noting that the transatlantic slave trade had been abolished, he describes the horrible internal slave trade, which was very much alive within the United States. The contrast between this description and what the Fourth of July is supposed to represent is stunning, as is Douglass's condemnation of the Fugitive Slave Law, which went into effect two years before this speech was delivered and required the return of runaway slaves, wherever found, to their owners. He also condemned one of his favorite targets, Christian churches that support slavery.

The point he drives home at the end of this blazing speech is that slavery is a threat to a unified United States, the implication being that if it is not destroyed, the United States will be. He contends also, in opposition to Garrison, that the Constitution is not proslavery. Taken altogether, this speech is one of the most powerful and effective attacks on slavery and racism ever given. It supports the claim that Douglass is the premiere abolitionist in American history.

The same year Douglass delivered his Fourth of July speech, 1852, Harriet Beecher Stowe published *Uncle Tom's Cabin*, which received positive reviews in *Frederick Douglass' Paper*. Douglass thought highly of Stowe's bestseller, but he did not envision the self-sacrificing figure of Uncle Tom himself as a model for black leadership against slavery and racism. In the 1850s Douglass continued to lecture and write: his lecture "The Claims of the Negro Ethnologically Considered" was delivered in 1854 at Western Reserve College (now Case Western Reserve University) as part of its graduation ceremonies that year. In it he argues for the self-evident humanity of everyone, regardless of physical characteristics.

In 1857, he published speeches on the Dred Scott decision (the Supreme Court ruled that year that a slave named Dred Scott could not become free by going into a state where slavery was illegal; Chief Justice Taney made the notorious statement that black people "had no rights which the white man was bound to respect"). Douglass saw an opportunity here. He made it very clear that if slavery was to ever end, it would have to be by force. As strong as the institution of slavery appears to be, Douglass noted, the abolitionists have not given up the fight to end it. Douglass also said that the Supreme Court does not have the power to overturn the Law of God, which Douglass believed endorsed the equality of everyone. He also warns his audience that for slavery to be abolished, the South may have to be subjected to catastrophic violence. He notes too that it would be a mistake for the North to secede from the Union as William Lloyd Garrison argued. If the North seceded, slaves would have no source of support. (However, the fact of the matter is that in 1857 the North was not giving slaves any support as far as the federal government was concerned. Northerners who assisted fugitive slaves did so in violation of federal law; if the North were a separate country, then it could at least in theory be a true haven for escaped slaves, much like Canada.) And Douglass is particularly concerned to argue that the Constitution is not proslavery, a position he did support when he was on the side of Garrisonian abolitionism. Douglass was not saying that the fugitive slave clause and the three-fifths clause (a slave represented three-fifths of a person when political representation was at stake) in the Dred Scott decision did not matter but that the Constitution was not proslavery ("slave" and "slavery" are not used in the Constitution), as the Dred Scott decision claimed. When Douglass became a political abolitionist instead of a Garrisonian abolitionist, he rejected Garrison's belief that the Constitution was a proslavery document, insisting that its general principle of freedom meant it was an antislavery document. In fact, brilliant thinkers like Douglass consider the Constitution to be a document that is ambiguous and not self-interpreting, which means that when conditions change, it can be interpreted so as to meet the critical needs of different times and places, a point that continues to cause consternation in twenty-first century America. In other words, while the black ink on the pages of the Constitution remains fairly constant, the readers of it change and thus read it differently from the way their predecessors do and successors will do.

In his speech celebrating West Indian emancipation, also delivered in 1857, Douglass raises the issue of why the freeing of slaves in the British West Indies in 1834 did not cause joy in the country of freedom, the United States. The answer is that many Americans doubted there was money to be made from the ending of slavery in the West Indies: financial greed was triumphant over moral principle, just as it had been in the slaveholding states of the United States. At the end of this speech, Douglas cites Madison Washington as someone American slaves should emulate, rather than waiting for help from nonslaves to end slavery. He is moving closer to endorsing violence to end slavery.

Two years after these speeches, Douglass became involved with John Brown, who stayed at Douglass's house in Rochester, New York, for a while. Douglass tried to dissuade Brown from attacking Harpers Ferry, but without success. He told Brown that he was "going into a perfect steel trap, and that once in he would not get out alive" (*Life and Times of Frederick Douglass*). But it was not Brown's use of violence that Douglass objected to; rather, he opposed the raid because it was doomed from the start. When Brown and his followers were captured by Federal troops led by Robert E. Lee, Douglass fled to Canada and then Great Britain because of his association with Brown, but he returned to the United States in April of 1860 because of the death of his daughter Annie. That same year he also delivered

This is Douglass at his most distinguished: well-dressed, handsome, and dignified. (Library of Congress)

a speech on self-made men, one he gave many times afterward because it was so popular.

In 1860 Douglass also supported Lincoln for president. The two self-made men had a complicated relationship, partly because Lincoln was a sometimes cautious politician, whereas Douglass was a relentless agitator who wanted to end slavery by whatever means necessary. Douglass was one of the first (nonservant) African Americans to visit the White House. He visited Lincoln three times and was well received. Douglass's account of Lincoln in *Life and Times* is often quoted: "Mr. Lincoln was not only a great President, but a great man—too great to be small in anything. In his company I was never in any way reminded of my humble origin, or of my unpopular color."

When the Civil War began in 1861, Douglass supported it and encouraged the use of slaves and free blacks in the Union army. At first Lincoln refused to endorse the idea, but with the Emancipation Proclamation of January 1, 1863, he agreed. The Proclamation freed slaves in Union-controlled ground in the Confederacy, not in areas controlled by Confederate troops. Douglass recruited for the 54th Massachusetts Infantry

Although Douglass thought Lincoln was too cautious in abolishing slavery, the two became friends. (Library of Congress)

Regiment and two of his sons, Charles Remond Douglass and Lewis Henry Douglass, joined it. As the first all-black unit in the Union army, except for officers above the rank of sergeant, it was watched carefully by white observers for signs of cowardice or ineptitude, but it fought bravely, particularly in the attack on Ft. Wagner in South Carolina in 1863. Though the 54th was turned back and suffered huge losses, it proved black troops were the equal of their white counterparts on the battlefield. Even though black units were paid less than white ones, and given jobs that involved tedious physical labor more often than white soldiers were, Douglass persevered in his push for more black troops; he also wrote an editorial entitled "Why Should a Colored Man Enlist" (1863) in which he made shrewd arguments to encourage the enlistment of black men: if you, a black man, are a man, you should choose to fight for the right side in a war between right and wrong; if the Federal government asks for your enlistment and you fail to do so, you are dishonoring it; third, you will be doing what your enemies do not want you to do; fourth, enlist because force of arms is the only way slavery will be ended; fifth, enlist because doing so will prove you are not members of a cowardly race, as your enemies have suggested; sixth, enlist to prove that you are as deserving of the rights of citizenship as anyone else; seventh, fight for the Union because doing so will enable you to regain lost respect; eighth, enlist because doing so will prevent the country from drifting back into proslavery compromise; ninth, enlist because slaves will be more likely to approach black units in the South than white ones and thereby join in the fight to end slavery.

Douglass also supported Lincoln for president in 1864 and attended his second inauguration. It was the first time in American history that an African American had been admitted to the White House for such an important function. Douglass described his visit as follows: "Like a mountain pine high above all others, Mr. Lincoln stood, in his grand simplicity, and home-like beauty. Recognizing me, even before I reached him, he exclaimed, so that all around could hear him, 'Here comes my friend Douglass.' Taking me by the hand, he said, 'I am glad to see you. I saw you in the crowd to-day, listening to my inaugural address; how did you like it?' I said, 'Mr. Lincoln, I must not detain you with my poor opinion, when there are thousands waiting to shake hands with you.' 'No, no,' he said, 'you must stop a little, Douglass; there is no man in the country whose opinion I value more than yours. I want to know what you think of it?' I replied, 'Mr. Lincoln, that was a sacred effort.'" The two met twice at the White House. Lincoln would have met with him a third time, but Douglass refused to break a previous engagement. After Lincoln's assassination in 1865, Mary Todd Lincoln had her husband's walking stick given to Douglass.

After Lincoln's assassination in 1865, Douglass realized that the next president, Andrew Johnson, was no friend to black Americans. Johnson was a racist who also hated the upper class of whites in the South. When Douglass and other black activists met with Johnson to discuss what needed to be done in the aftermath of the bloodiest war in United States history, they were treated very rudely, and while Johnson claimed he was pursuing the type of lenient (toward the exConfederates) policies that Lincoln wanted, the "Radical" Republicans in Congress would surely have begged to differ. We will never know what kind of Reconstruction President Lincoln would have led. But certainly President Lincoln was better aligned with the Congressional Republicans than President Johnson was. Douglass's view of Reconstruction, as in the case of his view of whether the Constitution was proslavery, was oxymoronic: on the one hand, he endorsed self-reliance and economic development for the newly freed slaves, but on the other, he realized that they would need federal support if their newly won civil rights were to be respected. This ability to believe opposing views is often found among brilliant minds, which the English Romantic poet John Keats called negative capability ("that is when man is capable of being in uncertainties, mysteries, doubts, without any irritable reaching after fact and reason"). Keats cites Shakespeare as a primary example. Douglass incorporates contradictions into a higher principle: what will enable newly emancipated slaves to compete with whites on a level playing field? Believing as he did that gaining the franchise would result in social equality for freed blacks (freed black men, that is, since black women did not have the right to vote during the Reconstruction period), Douglass was devastated by the sad end of Reconstruction in 1877, which disenfranchised black men, and thus their chance for social equality in the South. But the white South avoided treating black people with respect, as demonstrated by interfering with their right to vote and run for public office, for instance, until a century later. In the meantime, the Ku Klux Klan and other hate groups murdered and harassed the South's newest citizens, which forced Douglass to face the fact that ending slavery was one thing, social equality something else.

In 1876 he gave one of the most important speeches ever delivered anywhere or anytime. When Douglass says, in his 1876 speech, that Lincoln was "a white man's president," it should be noted that the phrase meant a very different thing in Lincoln's time, when only white men could vote and nonwhites had no representation. Every president before 1868 (or perhaps decades later, as it were) was a white man's president. Douglass in this speech simultaneously recognizes Lincoln as a man of his time, with all the prejudices and the narrow constituency that came with it, and as a man who often transcended his times. In that regard Douglass had the perspective of a historian. While it is true that Lincoln's focus before 1862 was entirely on preserving the Union, Douglass himself understood the political realities involved, as he stated in this speech: "Had he put the abolition of slavery before the salvation of the Union, he would have inevitably driven from him a powerful class of the American people and rendered resistance to rebellion impossible." Douglass also said of Lincoln in this speech that "[t]he man who could say [in his Second Inaugural Address], 'Fondly do we hope, fervently do we pray, that this mighty scourge of war shall soon pass away, yet if God wills it continue till all the wealth piled by two hundred years of bondage shall have been wasted, and each drop of blood drawn by the lash shall have been paid for by one drawn by the sword, the judgments of the Lord are true and righteous altogether' gives all needed proof of his feeling on the subject of slavery."

Douglass's 1876 speech was delivered in memory of Lincoln on April 14th, at the unveiling of the Freedman's Monument in Lincoln Park, Washington, D.C. It is balanced, with some harsh criticism in the first half before praising Lincoln in superlative terms in the second. Douglass's admiration for Lincoln was complicated but unmistakable, as his full speech makes clear; his ultimate assessment of Lincoln is positive. Douglass says in this speech that "when he [Lincoln] strangely told us [black people] that we were the cause of the war," he is referring to the following lines from the Second Inaugural Address: "These slaves constituted a peculiar and powerful interest. All knew that this interest was somehow the cause of the war." Here Lincoln seems to be blaming the institution of slavery, not the slaves themselves, though his syntax is odd. Douglass also criticizes Lincoln for his proposal to send blacks to Africa, which is monstrous today but of a piece with nineteenth-century colonization schemes that dated back to James Monroe's time, with the rationale that blacks would be better off in Africa because they could not get fair treatment from white Americans. Lincoln made that proposal as late as 1862, drawing a sharply negative reaction from Douglass and other black leaders. But despite Lincoln's copious flaws, Douglass and other blacks correctly saw in him a different kind of white politician, one who could eventually facilitate their emancipation.

It also needs to be kept in mind that even before Lincoln armed black troops or announced plans for emancipation, two of the historical developments that Douglass suggests could have happened sooner than they did, he and other black leaders were perceptive about the Lincoln of 1860–1861. It is easy for modern readers to look at Lincoln's 1860 platform and early statements in support of preserving slavery and the Union and be misled into thinking that he was proslavery and that blacks who had faith in him were fools. Yet Douglass and other blacks recognized that he was different; so did southern secessionists, in the opposite way. Prior to the 1860 election, Lincoln had publicly condemned slavery numerous times, said that the nation could not survive half slave and half free, and taken a resolute stance against slavery's expansion into the territories. In the final 1858 debate with Stephen Douglas, Lincoln approvingly used the phrase "ultimate extinction" ten times in connection with slavery, including this passage: "And whenever we can get rid of the fog which obscures the real question—when we can get Judge Douglas and his friends to avow a policy looking to its perpetuation—we can get out from among that class of men and bring them to the side of those who treat it as a wrong. Then there will soon be an end of it, and that end will be its 'ultimate extinction.'" While Lincoln was no abolitionist and early on even offered a constitutional amendment preserving slavery in the states that already had it, he was sufficiently anathema to the "white men" of those states that he was not even on the ballot in most of them and, of course, eleven of those states seceded from the Union rather than take their chances with Honest Abe. Lincoln's predecessors (Buchanan, Pierce, Fillmore) put the Union ahead of everything else and offered no resistance to the extension of slavery into the territories.

In the early 1870s Douglass and his family moved from Rochester to Washington, D.C. President Ulysses S. Grant appointed him to a commission that was charged with examining the annexation of the Dominican Republic, which Douglass supported. This decision has bothered many of Douglass's admirers, because it seems uncomfortably close to the great abolitionist's endorsing United States foreign policies that contradict his fight for justice and equality for African Americans. In the early 1870s, Douglass also became president of the Freedman's Savings Bank, a venture that failed. He lost a substantial sum himself when he tried to prop up an early attempt at helping black people participate in capitalism, a goal Douglass strongly supported. Douglass also lent his support to the cause of woman suffrage. Previously he had been criticized for supporting voting rights for black men but not for women, and he had said he was merely being politically realistic, but after the passage of the Fifteenth Amendment in 1870, which gave voting rights to all men, he reversed himself. In 1877, he was appointed U.S. Marshall of the District of Columbia, a position that required approval by the U.S. Senate. Douglass had come a very long way since his days as a fugitive slave.

His life continued to be an eventful one in the 1880s and '90s. President Garfield appointed him recorder of deeds for the District of Columbia in 1881, the same year he published the third version of his autobiography, *Life and Times of Frederick Douglass*. In 1882, his wife of forty-four years, Anna Murray Douglass, died. The couple had five children: three sons—Lewis Henry Douglass, Frederick Douglass Jr., and Charles Remond Douglass—and two daughters—Rosetta Douglass and Annie Douglass. Two years after his first wife's death, Douglass married a white woman names Helen Pitts; this marriage angered blacks and whites, especially Douglass's children and Helen Pitts's father, but the marriage prospered and she dedicated her life after Douglass's death to his memory and legacy. There were many other women in Douglass's life, including Julia Griffiths and Ottilie Assing. The former lived with the Douglasses for a while, helping edit Douglass's writings and publishing *Autographs for Freedom* (1854), which contained *The Heroic Slave*. After Douglass and William Lloyd Garrison went separate ways as abolitionists, Garrison charged that Douglass and Griffiths were in an adulterous relationship, although he had no evidence to support the claim. On the other hand, Douglass and Assing, it has been speculated, may have had an affair in the 1850s, which may have been connected to her suicide in 1884, when she read about Douglass's upcoming marriage to Helen Pitts.

In 1889, Douglass became the U.S. minister resident and consul general to Haiti, a position he resigned in 1891 because it became clear to Douglass that the United States was exploiting Haiti for economic purposes. The next year he was appointed commissioner of the Haitian pavilion at the World's Columbian Exposition in Chicago. The spirit of the firebrand Douglass reasserted itself because this exposition was designed to serve white interests, and thus there would be no African American presence to protest this absence. Douglass joined with Ida B. Wells (author of *A Red Record* who spent her life trying to get antilynching legislation passed at the federal level), Irvine Garland Penn (a black businessman), and Ferdinand L. Barnett (a black attorney who married Ida B. Wells) to produce a pamphlet entitled *The Reason Why the Colored American Is Not in the World's Columbian Exposition* (1893). In his introduction, Douglass observed that while American slavery had been destroyed, its spirit remained, which is the reason African Americans were excluded from the exposition. For a while after the Civil War, the North appreciated the contributions of black Americans to the South's defeat, but by 1892 that gratitude had been forgotten. The pamphlet demonstrated black people would nevertheless continue to insist on their importance to the United States.

In 1895, Douglass gave his last speech, and it was on women's rights; he died soon afterwards, possibly of a heart attack. But his legacy and claim as one of the two most important figures, along with Abraham Lincoln, in nineteenth-century American history are well established now. In a century of giants, Douglass continues to stand out.

CHAPTER 2

☙❧

Slavery in the Land of Freedom

The nineteenth century in the United States was a time continually leading to a second revolution, a new birth of freedom, which would narrow the gap between the promise and the reality of the American ideals of freedom and equality. Before the beginning of the Civil War in 1861, a small percentage of the population, comprised mostly of wealthy, educated white men, was more equal and freer than the rest of society. After 1865, when the Civil War ended, more men (and it was still largely men) had the chance to realize their potential, as Abraham Lincoln and Frederick Douglass did (both were, to a considerable extent, self-made men). For this change to occur, though, a tiny sliver of the white male elite had to be forced to give up their ownership of four million slaves. As Douglass noted, power never gives up power voluntarily. Before 1861, many attempts to maintain and destroy slavery were made, including continued violence against slaves, slave rebellions, written attacks on and in defense of slavery, speeches, the Underground Railroad, antislavery societies, and political and legal maneuvering. But in every attempt the question at issue was the same: do Americans born into privilege have a ticket to ride on the backs of those who were not?

From the beginning of legal slavery through the Civil War, it was, and had to be, maintained by violence. Otherwise, the slaves would have overthrown the system. Whipping, scourging, and flogging were a common punishment, as was maiming by cutting off ears, fingers, hands, and feet. Slaves were hit, beaten, hanged, shot, and imprisoned; some were torn to bits by hounds. Other slaves were killed or suspended by their thumbs. But slaves continued to resist by breaking tools, feigning illness, slowing down work, destroying tools, and of course by running away. They could also fight back, as Douglass did against Mr. Covey, and plan violent insurrections.

Despite some famous slave uprisings, they appear to have been few in number. Slave uprisings and escapes were so uncommon for good reason. Fans of the "Magnolia myth" would say it was because slaves were contented, but historians seem to agree that it was because of the threat of severe punishment (from death to forced sales of family members) and the minimal chance of success, as they were up against a vast police state. In 1800, Gabriel Prosser organized a large-scale attempt to overthrow the masters in Richmond, Virginia, and other nearby cities. A large black man of keen intelligence, Prosser was literate and a blacksmith allowed to hire out his labors. A very heavy rainstorm and betrayal by several other slaves doomed his planned insurrection, but it did frighten whites into the realization that slaves were capable of the same kind of resistance to slavery whites would have engaged in had they been enslaved. The rainstorm forced Prosser to postpone the attack on Richmond, which gave whites time to begin to search out, find, and hang many of the rebels, including their leader, although Prosser did manage to avoid capture for a while. In the early twenty-first century, Virginia pardoned Gabriel Prosser and acknowledged that he and his followers were acting in the hallowed American tradition of being willing to fight for their freedom. And in 1936, Arna Bontemps published a novel inspired by Prosser's insurrection, *Black Thunder*.

About twenty years after Gabriel Prosser's planned rebellion, Denmark Vesey, a free black man who used his winnings from a lottery to buy himself out of slavery, planned to overthrow slavery in Charleston, South Carolina. How many black people were willing to join his conspiracy is subject to debate, but it may have been substantial. Apparently, Vesey planned to kill as many slaveowners as possible and then sail to Haiti with his followers. After several slaves informed on Vesey before the insurrection was launched, he and several followers were hanged, but Vesey's attempted conspiracy nevertheless is more evidence that slaves were anything but happy, and some realized violence was the only way slavery was going to be destroyed. There is a statue of Denmark Vesey in Charleston now, but it is far outnumbered by the monuments to whites who fought in a war to perpetuate slavery.

The best known slave insurrection was led by Nat Turner in 1831. It inspired William Styron's controversial novel, *The Confessions of Nat Turner* (1967) and figures prominently in Harriet Jacobs's *Incidents in the Life of a Slave Girl* (1861). A religious visionary, Turner and his men killed sixty white people, including children, women, and men, in Southampton, Virginia. The white reaction was to kill far more blacks, many of whom had nothing to do with the rebellion. Turner managed to escape capture at first, but he was eventually found and hanged. A white attorney named Thomas Grey interviewed Turner and published a pamphlet entitled *The Confessions of Nat Turner* (1831). Grey's publication depicted Turner as a deluded fanatic, a representation that partially reassured whites that slaves were not capable of revolting against slavery the way whites would have been. It was even suggested that a white man in black face was the real instigator of the rebellion. Actually, Turner was a bright, capable leader who was well aware of what he was doing.

Slave rebellions on board slave ships had better chances of success because the slaves outnumbered the white crew and because the whites obviously could not call for reinforcement at sea. The best known slave revolt at sea took place on the *Amistad* (a Spanish word that ironically means friendship) in 1839; led by a slave named Joseph Cinqué, the fifty-three Africans killed two of the crew and demanded that the survivors take them back to Africa, but the surviving crew members steered the *Amistad* in an easterly direction during the day (the ship had left Havana), and back toward the northeastern United States at night. A United States warship captured the ship off of Long Island. The legal case surrounding the question of what to do with the Africans gained international attention: the Spanish owner wanted his "property" back, but the Supreme Court ruled that the Africans were free. The *Amistad* took on symbolic overtones as to what needed to be done to destroy slavery; it became a touchstone for abolitionists in their efforts to prevail against it.

The slave uprising that particularly interested Frederick Douglass occurred on board the *Creole* in 1841. It was supposed to sail from Richmond, Virginia, to New Orleans, where slave trading was extremely profitable. By 1841, the international slave trade was illegal in the United States, but not the internal slave trade. On board the *Creole* was a recaptured slave named Madison Washington, who had left Canada to find his wife Susan; what was unknown to both, as black women and black men were kept in different parts of the ship, was that each was on the *Creole*; after the revolt, the two were reunited. The slaves freed themselves and overcame the American crew. Madison Washington is said to have been adamant in his demand that the killing be kept to the minimum and that freedom, not revenge, be understood as the uprising's goal. The *Creole* then sailed for Nassau, in the Bahamas, where the then-British rule did not recognize slavery as legal, so most of the Africans gained their freedom. Douglass may well have seen himself in Madison Washington, whom he tried to find without success; Douglass saw him as a model black hero who used violence, like the white Americans in 1776, to gain freedom from tyranny. Douglass invented the character Listwell in *The Heroic Slave*, Madison Washington's friend, to serve as an example of how white abolitionists could help slaves gain their freedom.

The best known attempt to destroy slavery through violence before the Civil War was not at sea but on land: John Brown's unsuccessful raid on Harpers Ferry in 1859, just two years before the war started. Although the raid, which Brown envisioned as just the beginning of a massive slave insurrection, was suppressed by Federal troops under the command of then-Lieutenant Colonel Robert E. Lee, it nevertheless sparked the imagination of southerners and northerners: white southerners feared that Brown's raid might be just the beginning of an attempt to overthrow slavery by force of arms; some northerners saw it as a brave and heroic attempt, however doomed, to end slavery. As polarizing as Brown's raid was, we should be careful not to overgeneralize about how southerners and northerners felt about slavery and abolition. It must be remembered that much of the southern population was black, and that much, perhaps most, of the northern white population was not only racist but entirely willing to tolerate slavery. Northern Presidents Fillmore, Pierce, and Buchanan were proslavery in their actions if not in their personal beliefs. In the 1860s there were proslavery "Copperheads" and racist draft rioters in the North. Brown urged Douglass himself to join in the attack, but out of fear or discretion or both, as Douglass admitted in *The Life and Times of Frederick Douglass* (1881), he did not go with Brown, although he always thought and spoke very highly of him, regarding him as a martyr to the abolitionist cause. It is extremely fortunate Douglass did not take part, because he would certainly have been hanged if he had. Douglass had allowed Brown to stay with him in his house in Rochester, New York, and consequently after the raid he wisely fled to Canada and then to England, as he knew he would be arrested and executed if he were apprehended.

The ultimate act of violence against slavery was the Civil War (1861–1865). Lincoln was careful to make sure the Confederacy fired the first shot, which occurred at Fort Sumter in South Carolina in April 1861. At the beginning of the war Lincoln emphasized that his goal was to preserve the Union, but by 1862 he realized that to accomplish that goal, he would have to destroy slavery because it was the bedrock of the Confederacy's economy. While the Emancipation Proclamation was officially issued on January 1, 1863, Lincoln had written a draft of it by the summer of 1862 and had announced on September 22, 1862, that all slaves in rebel states would be emancipated as of January 1. By the middle of the war, Lincoln also accepted Douglass's advice to use black troops (toward the end of the war, the Confederacy also considered this idea), and approximately 200,000 black men did fight for the Union; it is possible the Union would have lost without them.

When the war began, many white people in the Union and the Confederacy thought it would be over in a few months, with only a few casualties. Four years and approximately 750,000 deaths later, it finally ended with the devastating and bitter defeat of the Confederacy. But while it lost the war on the battlefield, it won the racial war, and this for another century and more. The former slave was a convenient target of white revenge and anger. Many white southerners started spreading the "Lost Cause" myth (see Edward A. Pollard, *The Lost Cause*, 1866) shortly after the war ended. According to this myth, the Civil War was about states' rights, not slavery. But the Confederate Declarations of Secession typically referred explicitly to slavery's preservation, not states' rights, as the reason for secession. There was also a clear pattern of states with the most slaves (as percent of the population) seceding earliest. The Civil War destroyed slavery as a legal system of exploitation, but it did not destroy its new form: African Americans in the South and North had to continue their fight for real freedom, a fight still underway over a century after the war ended.

The attempts to perpetuate and destroy slavery also included a war of words written and spoken. Slave narratives were among the most powerful attacks on slavery: Douglass's first autobiography is the most famous, but William Wells Brown and Solomon Northup also produced notable life stories of their own. Brown's *Narrative of William Wells Brown, A Fugitive Slave: Written by Himself,* appeared two years after Douglass's first autobiography was published in 1845. Brown was so grateful to a Quaker named Wells Brown who helped him when he escaped to Canada that he took the man's name. Brown worked at many different jobs after his escape from slavery in 1834 and became literate and well read, as he, too, like Douglass, showed what black men could accomplish, contrary to the expectations of many whites, if given the chance.

Solomon Northup dedicated his bestselling slave narrative to Harriet Beecher Stowe and published it the year after *Uncle Tom's Cabin* was published in 1852. Northup was a free black man and an accomplished fiddle player who attracted the attention of two con artists who promised him money if he would go into business with them. Instead, they drugged him and sold him into slavery. Much of Northup's autobiography is concerned with the legal machinations he went through to regain his freedom. Like William Wells Brown's autobiography, *Twelve Years a Slave* makes a powerful case against slavery through the resourcefulness and determination of a hero who refuses to accept his enslavement.

Many novels, antislavery and proslavery, were written in the war of words slavery provoked. *Uncle Tom's Cabin*, the most famous and best selling, is said to have caused President Lincoln to exclaim to its author that she caused the Civil War. Whatever the case, Stowe's novel did bring tears to the eyes of many northern white readers (it sold 300,000 copies, a huge number for a nineteenth-century American book). The depiction of Uncle Tom as a saintly, non-sexual man of peace and benevolence, who completely rejected violence, was designed to enlist readers in the cause of abolishing slavery, and it did. Stowe played very strongly on the sympathies of northern wives and mothers in her treatment of the slave Eliza jumping from one block of ice to another on the Ohio River to escape, with her little girl, from slave hunters. What many modern-day readers condemn as melodramatic language, plot, and characters, Stowe used intentionally because she knew her readers in 1852 would find it irresistible.

Harriet Jacobs knew that, too, as her *Incidents in the Life of a Slave Girl* (1861) makes clear. A combination of the novel of romance and a slave narrative, Jacobs's book tells the story of her fifteen-year-old self resisting the relentless sexual harassment of her middle-aged owner, called Dr. Flint. He offers to make her a "lady" with her own cottage in the woods, if she will acquiesce to his plan. Jacobs hoped sisterhood would trump racism in her appeal to white northern wives and mothers' own experience with sexual pressure and exploitation. She also represented her younger self as capable of resisting the tyranny of slavery by at least being able to choose her lover, thereby rejecting Dr. Flint, which resulted in her gaining a substantial victory over him. Bold and outspoken for its time, *Incidents in the Life of a Slave Girl* indicates that there are ways to resist slavery, no matter how overwhelming its power may have seemed.

Numerous proslavery novels also appeared, including William Gilmore Simms's *The Sword and the Distaff: Or, Fair, Fat, and Forty: A Story of the South, at the Close of the Revolution.* Published the same year as *Uncle Tom's Cabin* (1852), Simms's novel was part of what is now looked on as "anti-Tom" literature, work written to challenge Stowe's representation of slavery and combat her influence, although it is possible Simms was not thinking of *Uncle Tom's Cabin* when he wrote *The Sword and the Distaff*, which in any case presents slavery from a sympathetic point of view.

In the case of Caroline Lee Hentz's *The Planter's Northern Bride* (1854), however, there is no doubt her targets are Stowe's novel and abolitionism. Convinced that most of the slaves were content and loyal to their owners, Hentz views abolitionists as wild and dangerous fanatics, while Russell Moreland, the planter of the title, is benign and deeply concerned for his slaves, who return his affection for them. Hentz used the same literary conventions Harriet Jacobs used in *Incidents in the Life of a Slave Girl*, melodrama and emotional appeals, but for very different ends. Similarly, *Aunt Phillis's Cabin; or Southern Life as It Is* (1852), by Mary Eastman, is also an attack on Stowe's novel, as Eastman quotes from it in her novel and is obviously trying to correct what she regards as misrepresentations of slavery: she argues that slaves are better off than the white working class in the North because the former are never faced with the problems of unemployment.

John Pendleton Kennedy's *Swallow Barn or A Sojourn in the Old Dominion* (1832) contains mixed feelings about slavery. It views plantation life in Virginia with some nostalgia, but it also acknowledges slavery is wrong. Kennedy indicates that slaves are content by nature, though, and also going to be dependent on whites whether they are emancipated or sent back to Africa. To Kennedy's credit, he eventually became an abolitionist after hearing a speech by Douglass and helped to bring about the end of slavery in Maryland, where the Emancipation Proclamation did not apply because it was not part of the Confederacy.

In oratory, too, numerous attempts to end and perpetuate slavery were made in a century known for great speeches. One of the most powerful speeches delivered against slavery was that by Henry Highland Garnet (1815–1892). A Presbyterian minister and abolitionist, Garnet was more radical than Douglass when he gave this speech in 1843, because Garnet endorsed the concept of ending slavery by any means necessary, while Douglass was still taking the position of nonviolent moral persuasion then. The speech, "An Address to the Slaves of the United States," did not quite succeed in being endorsed by the National Negro Convention; Douglass voted against it. Referred to as the "Call to Rebellion" speech, Garnet's address targets the slaves, rather than black people in the North. He insists that they have an obligation to overthrow the system of slavery by whatever means are found necessary. He adds that the hardship of rebellion can hardly be greater than what his intended audience has already faced as slaves.

Phillips was the second best-known abolitionist in the nineteenth century. (Library of Congress)

Echoing Patrick Henry, Garnet goes on to remind enslaved black people that it is obvious that liberty should be their goal. If the slaves revolt, they will join the likes of Denmark Vesey and George Washington in their quest for freedom. Garnet also praises Joseph Cinqué and Madison Washington, black men who led successful revolts on slave ships, his point being that slaves will be joining in a well established tradition of organized black violence against slavery, if they rise up against their masters in the South. Reminding them that there are four million slaves in the South in 1843, he claims there has never been a better time to revolt. At the end of his address, Garnet appeals to their sense of manhood: how much longer are you willing to submit to the sexual exploitation of your wives by white men?

Wendell Phillips, one of the leading white abolitionists, gave many speeches arguing for the destruction of slavery. One of the most stirring was his defense of an abolitionist editor named Elijah Lovejoy, who was murdered by a mob in Alton, Illinois, in 1837. After the attorney general of Massachusetts gave a speech praising this act and comparing the mob to American patriots in the Revolution, Phillips stood up and challenged the audience's support of what the attorney general had said. The setting was Faneuil Hall, in Boston. At first the crowd rejected the 26-year-old Phillips's speech but then shifted its position because Phillips was so persuasive. Pointing out that Lovejoy and his supporters fired only after the mob had fired at them, Phillips also noted that Lovejoy was a martyr to free speech, while the mob opposed that freedom. He also shrewdly declared that white self-interest, in 1776, meant nonpayment of taxes to the British government; Lovejoy's case concerned a higher principle, opposing censorship of free speech. This talk launched Phillips's lifelong career as an advocate for the abolition of slavery and for the establishment of women's rights.

The most famous white abolitionist was William Lloyd Garrison (1805–1879). He dedicated most of his adult life to the cause of abolition and kept his newspaper, *The Liberator*, going for over thirty years, a remarkable feat when so many abolitionist newspapers struggled to survive. His most famous speech, "No Compromise with the Evil of Slavery," was delivered in 1854, when civil war was looming. He begins by pointing to the contradiction between the Declaration of Independence and slavery: if all men are created equal, then there can be no slaves. If anyone can convince him that slavery is right, he will disavow his belief in the Declaration. But he does not know how freedom and slavery can coexist. If Americans will not abolish slavery, then they should give up talk about the rights of man. Furthermore, Garrison holds that abolition should be absolute and subject to no compromise whatsoever. If slaves are not human, then they should not go to church or be taught the catechism. But if they are human, they should be emancipated immediately and unconditionally. He also argues that the North has put maintaining the Union over all other considerations, including abolition, while the South has put slavery's survival over everything else. And then he concludes with a rousing cry for, regardless of the consequences, the end of slavery. Garrison actually called for the *North* to leave the Union—"no union with slaveholders" was his rallying cry—and he believed northern secession would bring an end to slavery. His rationale was that the Union would be a haven for escaped slaves, that there would be diminished government support for quelling slave insurrection, and that there would be diminished slave-state claims on new territories (Henry Mayer, *All on Fire: William Lloyd Garrison and the Abolition of Slavery*, New York: St. Martin's Press, 1998, p. 452). The idea was that slavery would have withered away, as more and more slaves escaped or rebelled. The opposing agreement, that northern secession would have preserved slavery, presumably assumed the slave states would set up a more comprehensive police state of their own.

White southern voices were raised also, but in defense of slavery, two of the most notable being James Henry Hammond's and John C. Calhoun's. The former, a wealthy plantation owner and United States senator, delivered his speech on the so-called mudsill theory to the Senate in 1858. Hammond claimed that every society required a mudsill, that is, a base, for the upper class. The white South, therefore, needed black people as the foundation for the planter aristocracy, which was doing what was only "natural" in accepting this arrangement, because blacks were docile and unable to care for themselves, whereas in the North, the laboring class, which was white, resented being what amounts to slaves, in Hammond's judgment. John C. Calhoun (1782–1850), twice vice-president and senator from South Carolina, declared in his most famous speech to the Senate, delivered in 1837, that not only was slavery not an evil, but a positive good, because it was the basis for a "natural" and stable relationship between blacks and whites in the South. He acknowledged his fear that the deranged fanaticism of the abolitionists, as he saw them, and the complacency of many white southerners, could result in war between the two main sections of the country. His position was in the minds of South Carolinians who seceded from the United States in 1861.

In addition to all these attempts to end and support slavery, many newspapers were also founded to serve each cause. By far the most famous newspaper devoted to destroying or perpetuating slavery was William Lloyd Garrison's abolitionist *The Liberator* (1831–1865); only a few thousand people subscribed, including African Americans, but it had a substantial impact. The main criticism was that Garrison, while always determined and outspoken, did not offer practical ways to bring about emancipation; moral persuasion alone was not enough to abolish slavery. But he always stood by his opening statement in the first issue: "I am in earnest—I will not equivocate—I will not excuse—I will not retreat a single inch—AND I WILL BE HEARD."

Frederick Douglass was also a key figure in the history of abolitionist newspapers with his *The North Star*, named after the star escaped slaves followed on their journey north. Garrison felt betrayed by Douglass's independence and never forgave him for going his own way. Douglass rejected Garrisonian abolitionism, based on moral suasion, in favor of political abolitionism, based on using politics to end slavery. Douglass was unusual in his belief that Lincoln could be turned into a political abolitionist, which meant Lincoln might support emancipation, which he did in his preliminary proclamation of September 1862. The Emancipation Proclamation itself was announced on January 1, 1863. That is when Douglass realized he and Lincoln were walking on the same path, because freeing the slaves in areas of the Confederacy controlled by Union forces meant the Confederacy was doomed. It seems unlikely that Douglass knew in advance that he and Lincoln would come to be as one in their political and military views, but he may have sensed Lincoln's potential for change and growth. The motto of *The North Star* was "Right is of no sex—Truth is of no color—God is the Father of us all, and we are brethren." Constantly faced with financial difficulties, *The North Star* eventually merged with the white abolitionist Gerrit Smith's *Liberty Party Paper* to become *Frederick Douglass' Paper.*

Among the anti-abolitionist newspapers, *The Cincinnati Post and Anti-Abolitionist* and the *Kansas Weekly Herald* are worth noting. The former had only a brief run (1841–1842), but it did publish the names of abolitionists in Cincinnati to put pressure on them to desist. Included were Lyman Beecher, Harriet Beecher Stowe's father, who had moved to Cincinnati to head Lane Theological Seminary, and Calvin Stowe, who taught at the seminary and married Harriet Beecher. The *Kansas Weekly Herald* (1854–1858) was caught up in the bitter, sometimes violent controversy over slavery in the Kansas territory. At times it took a strong pro-slavery position, arguing like John C. Calhoun, that slavery was not only not evil, but a positive good.

The legal cause of much of all the debate and violence concerning slavery in the nineteenth century was the decision made in the Constitutional Convention in 1787 to allow each state to have the right to regulate slavery, thus guaranteeing a never-resolved problem of states rights vs. federal rights. From Gabriel Prosser's intended rebellion in 1800 to the beginning of the Civil War in 1861, the question of who had the last say over slavery was argued back and forth between the North and the white South, with the masters claiming they had the right to do whatever they wanted with their human chattel and the North gradually moving toward the position that slavery had to be destroyed if the so-called United States was to survive.

As slavery steadily disappeared in the North, New Jersey having abolished it in 1804 for instance, it grew in the South to the point that by 1861, there were approximately four million slaves in what was then called the Confederacy, except for the states below the Mason-Dixon Line that did not join the Confederacy. While the external slave trade had ended, at least officially, in 1808, the internal slave trade flourished. By 1860, the market value of slaves was equal to roughly three-fourths of U.S. GDP, which meant that the planter aristocracy had absolutely no intention of freeing their slaves, regardless of what the federal government decreed.

The Underground Railroad and antislavery societies both helped to undermine slavery. The Underground Railroad was a loose, decentralized network of myriad escape routes. Even calling it a "network" overstates the degree of organization (see Eric Foner, *Gateway to Freedom* [2015]). It was neither underground nor a railroad; instead, it was a network of "stations" whereby fleeing slaves could escape from the South and end up in the North or Canada. Harriet Tubman was one of the more notable slaves who "got on board." The antislavery societies helped to focus attention in the North on a subject many northerners would otherwise have continued to ignore. The best known was William Lloyd Garrison's American Anti-Slavery Society, which was active from the early 1830s through 1870. It demanded the end of slavery by peaceful means, and for a while Douglass, who became one of its best known speakers, agreed with this policy.

The political and legal maneuverings included the Missouri Compromise of 1820 that allowed Missouri to enter the country as a slave state but also admitted Maine, then part of Massachusetts, as a free state. The Compromise maintained the balance between slave and free states at twelve each. Basically, the law put a patch over the boiling issue of whether slavery should be restricted to the South or allowed to expand. The planter aristocracy favored the latter course, northern whites the former. Thomas Jefferson feared for the fate of the United States as the problem of the expansion of slavery was left to new states to decide. The slaves themselves, as usual, had no say in the matter whatsoever. The Missouri Compromise postponed a civil war but did not prevent it.

From 1836 until 1844, the House of Representatives was under the Gag Rule. It prevented the consideration of any petition about slavery brought before the House. The American Anti-Slavery Society had submitted many such petitions, which led to the further outrage in the North about slavery, because many northerners believed in the Constitution's granting American citizens the right to petition for a redress of grievances. John Quincy Adams, a former president, led the fight in the House against the Gag Rule; he finally got it overturned in 1844. Representatives from slave states argued that Congress had no authority to examine the property rights of southern slaveholders. Northerners regarded the rule as an infringement on freedom of speech and thus strongly supported Adams. The Gag Rule controversy widened the split between the South and the North over slavery (some of the unread petitions called for the end of slavery in Washington, D.C.).

Two years after the Gag Rule ended in 1844, another development further increased tension between the North and the South over slavery: the Wilmot Proviso. David Wilmot was a member of the House of Representatives from Pennsylvania. Because he opposed the extension of slavery into the territory the United States was going to gain from the Mexican-American War (1846–1849), he attached a rider to the bill enabling President James K. Polk to negotiate with Mexico over the ceding of Mexican territory to the United States. This rider passed the House several times but was voted down by the Senate. Northerners and southerners were both angry over the dispute because the North feared the extension of slavery into new territories and the masters supported it. This rift moved the country closer to civil war. But it was really the Mexican War (1846–1848), not the Wilmot Proviso, that was at the heart of the surge in sectional tensions over slavery in the 1840s. Expansion of slavery had always been a contentious issue, one that the Missouri Compromise of 1820 papered over. With all the new territory gained in the Mexican War, though, there was the question of how much of it would be open to slavery. It is certainly notable that Wilmot's rider, banning slavery entirely in the new territories, passed the House three times, although any solution would have been controversial, as became clear in 1850.

What postponed the coming sectional bloodshed was the Compromise of 1850, which included the notorious Fugitive Slave Law. The masters thought this act would perpetuate slavery, but it led instead to its destruction. The bill required northerners to return runaway slaves to their owners. Penalties for noncompliance were stiff: a marshal or deputy marshal who refused to obey the law could be fined a thousand dollars, a very substantial sum in 1850. A citizen who interfered with the return of a fugitive slave could be sentenced to six months in jail. The slightest reason for calling any black person a fugitive slave was acceptable "evidence" for claiming that person as a slave. No black people captured could testify in their own defense. The law applied to all the states and territories. Officials involved in determining if a black person was an escaped slave received ten dollars if the accused was "proved" (that is, deemed) to be a fugitive, five dollars if not. In other words, anyone could make five dollars just by claiming a black person was a runaway. People who helped officials return fugitive slaves to their owners were also to be paid for their services. The Act basically increased obstacles for runaway slaves, increased penalties for their abettors, and helped enable the enslavement or re-enslavement of free blacks. The existence of this act suggests that slave escapes had become a big problem in the eyes of slaveholders. Some historians put fugitive slaves at the center of the sectional crisis over slavery, so an understanding of its importance is essential in studying nineteenth-century United States history.

The Fugitive Slave Law sparked outrage in the North. Whereas most northern whites had been indifferent to slavery in the South, after 1850 they realized they were directly implicated in it because they were legally required to obey the new law. Many northerners reacted loudly and angrily: refusing to submit to it, Ralph Waldo Emerson was appalled, saying it was beyond belief that such a law could be passed in the nineteenth century and by people who could read and write. Thoreau declared that the United States should be broken up; John Greenleaf Whittier condemned Daniel Webster, U.S. Senator from Massachusetts, for supporting it; Lincoln, on the other hand, supported it, and it was in effect even after the Emancipation Proclamation, which did not apply to the border states, like Maryland, a state that fought for the Union but had slaves.

The Kansas-Nebraska Act of 1854 made matters even worse. Sponsored by Stephen A. Douglas of Illinois, it repealed the Missouri Compromise of 1820; that compromise had maintained an uneasy peace between North and South for thirty-four years. Douglas was interested in the construction of a railroad across the rapidly growing country, one that would start in Chicago. Doing so required the establishment of territories, which could then become states admitted to the country. Southern interests would be threatened if Kansas and Nebraska were admitted as non-slave states, so Douglas said the matter would be decided by "popular sovereignty," which meant the (white males of the) states would vote to determine their status as slave or nonslave. But that meant the end of the 36°30 ' boundary as the northernmost border of slave states. Settlers rushed into the Kansas territory to determine its eventual admission to the Union as a free state or slave state. Conflicts between pro- and antislavery settlers quickly led to chronic violence. "Bleeding Kansas" predated the Civil War by six years, but in a sense it was the war's first installment.

Three years after the Kansas-Nebraska Act was passed, Supreme Court Chief Justice Roger B. Taney and six other judges made what is widely viewed today as the Supreme Court's worst decision: it ruled that a slave named Dred Scott could not sue his owner for release from slavery because black people had no rights that a white man was bound to respect. People of African descent were not citizens of the United States; therefore, Dred Scott could not file a suit to begin with. And the Court ruled the Missouri Compromise was unconstitutional, so Congress could not outlaw slavery in the territories. Taney's court also ruled that slaves brought into territories, as Scott had been, could not be freed. The North was furious about Taney's decision; Douglass gave a powerful speech condemning it in 1857. He pointed out that the slaveowners were more determined than ever to hold on to their human chattel and that it would be a grave mistake for the North to follow Garrison's idea that it should secede from the Union, because in Douglass's view that would make the survival of slavery more likely. Douglass's position is still argued about now. In any case, Douglass proclaimed that Taney's decision meant the day of reckoning would soon be at hand, and in this Douglass was right, as the Civil War began four years after Taney's notorious blunder.

The year after the Dred Scott decision, 1858, was the year the famous Lincoln-Douglas debates were held throughout Illinois. Stephen A. Douglas was running against Abraham Lincoln for re-election to the U.S. Senate, and while Douglas won the election (voted on by state legislatures then rather than directly by popular vote), Lincoln got the best of him in the debates and gained so much national prominence from his performance that he was nominated for the Republican candidate for president in 1860. Lincoln made it clear to more Americans than ever before that a house divided cannot stand: it cannot be both free and enslaved. He also condemned slavery when he approvingly speaks of its "ultimate extinction" ten times in the final debate. But Lincoln could not have hurt Douglas much, as Douglas won the election. Very, very few white Americans, including northern whites, were abolitionists at the time (just 2–5 percent, by historian Lee Benson's estimate), so Douglas's willingness to countenance slavery in the territories probably would not have hurt him much politically. Besides, Douglas's position was consistent with his longtime "popular sovereignty" advocacy.

Events of the utmost importance occurred between 1858 and 1863, including the election of Lincoln to the presidency, an election the masters correctly perceived as a possibly mortal threat to their way of life. So fearful were they that their world was coming to an end that they not only supported the secession of eleven states from the United States but also a war against what remained of it when the Confederacy was established. The Confederate declarations of secession were based on the masters' belief that wealthy plantation owners had the right to do what they wanted to do with their slaves: they sensed Lincoln believed instead in a democracy in which men should have equal opportunity to rise in the world, as he himself had. Lincoln personified what they feared most, freedom and equal opportunity. The resulting war was about democracy versus its opposite.

The two key legal documents in the numerous attempts to perpetuate or destroy slavery were the Emancipation Proclamation, issued January 1, 1863, and the Thirteenth Amendment. In this famous decree, Lincoln said the slaves in the states that had seceded were free, but he did not free the slaves in the proslavery northern border states, which had not seceded; that happened later. Slaves who crossed Union lines in Confederate states were declared free, and slaves were also offered the chance to join the Union army and navy. Approximately 200,000 did so. That meant not only more soldiers for the North but also fewer slaves supporting the Confederacy by maintaining plantations and working in munitions factories. Preserving the Union and destroying slavery had been officially recognized. The Thirteenth Amendment ("Neither slavery nor involuntary servitude, except as a punishment for crime whereof the party shall have been duly convicted, shall exist in the United States, or any place subject to their jurisdiction") was passed by the Senate in 1864, by the House in 1865; it deserves equal billing with the Emancipation Proclamation because it made emancipation permanent and included the non-Confederate slave states and all the other states.

The abolition of slavery did not mean true liberty for the exslaves. They had, for instance, to contend with the crop lien system (it should be noted that there were many white tenant farmers subject to crop liens as well), an arrangement by which tenants and sharecroppers borrowed supplies from merchants who held a lien on their crops until they were repaid. If the price of cotton or some other crop was low, the tenants and sharecroppers were in the red at the beginning of the next planting season. But there was much more to the sharecropper/tenant system than just the crop lien: Jim Crow (laws intended to support segregation, such as the use of "colored" drinking fountains for black people), lynching (a terror tactic designed to intimidate black people into submission to white control; Ida B. Wells in *A Red Record* is particularly helpful in understanding lynching), the Klan (a white hate group that used violence to terrify African Americans), vagrancy laws (laws that were thinly veiled excuses to force exslaves who might be trying to find lost family members, for instance, into employment), convict lease labor (the lease of convicts to companies by states to increase annual revenues), and discrimination against blacks for skilled work in the South and up North, meant a hardscrabble existence for most African Americans for many decades to come. Under that system, black sharecroppers and tenant farmers had virtually no other economic opportunities. Still, although African Americans in the South faced severe legal and social obstacles to basic liberties for a century after emancipation, none of them would have traded places with a slave. The value of freedom was considerable, even when that freedom was far from complete.

CЗ

Narrative of the Life of Frederick Douglass, an American Slave.

Written by Himself.[1]

BOSTON
PUBLISHED AT THE ANTI-SLAVERY OFFICE,
NO. 25 CORNHILL
1845
ENTERED, ACCORDING TO ACT OF CONGRESS,
IN THE YEAR 1845
BY FREDERICK DOUGLASS,
IN THE CLERK'S OFFICE OF THE DISTRICT COURT
OF MASSACHUSETTS.

---

1. The title of Douglass's autobiography is provocative: how can there be, in the land of freedom, a slave and slavery? That there is any need to counter doubts about its authorship is also revealing; it would be odd if Herman Melville had published his most famous novel under the rubric, *Moby Dick, Written by Melville Himself*, because no one would have doubted he wrote it. Douglass also wanted to react to the claim, sometimes true, that a slave narrative was written by a white author or dictated to a white writer by a slave.

Preface[2]

IN the month of August, 1841, I[3] attended an anti-slavery convention in Nantucket, at which it was my happiness to become acquainted with *Frederick Douglass*, the writer of the following Narrative. He was a stranger to nearly every member of that body; but, having recently made his escape from the southern prison-house of bondage, and feeling his curiosity excited to ascertain the principles and measures of the abolitionists,—of whom he had heard a somewhat vague description while he was a slave,—he was induced to give his attendance, on the occasion alluded to, though at that time a resident in New Bedford.

Fortunate, most fortunate occurrence!—fortunate for the millions of his manacled brethren, yet panting for deliverance from their awful thraldom!—fortunate for the cause of negro emancipation, and of universal liberty!—fortunate for the land of his birth, which he has already done so much to save and bless!—fortunate for a large circle of friends and acquaintances, whose sympathy and affection he has strongly secured by the many sufferings he has endured, by his virtuous traits of character, by his ever-abiding remembrance of those who are in bonds, as being bound with them!—fortunate for the multitudes, in various parts of our republic, whose minds he has enlightened on the subject of slavery, and who have been

---

2. By including a Preface by William Lloyd Garrison, Douglass further added to the book's authority because Garrison reinforces the idea that Douglass wrote it; and as the foremost white abolitionist, Garrison also adds credibility and prestige to Douglass's narrative: if a white man backs up Douglass's claims, they must be true. Garrison was of great historical significance because of his absolutely relentless attack on slavery. As cofounder of the American Anti-Slavery Society and editor of the most prominent abolitionist newspaper, *The Liberator*, he influenced many white northerners to wake up to the fact that they lived in a country where a large part of it embraced slavery, a morally intolerable situation; he also had tremendous influence on the young Frederick Douglass, convincing him that the Constitution was pro-slavery and slavery should be abolished through moral suasion, two views Douglass would later reject. Garrison and Douglass engaged in a speaking tour together that further spread Garrison's fame and influence.

3. William Lloyd Garrison. In 1845 Douglass looked up to Garrison almost as a father figure (Douglass tended to idolize some older adults he liked, perhaps in part because they represented the father and mother he never really had). As time passed, though, Douglass and Garrison had a vicious falling out, Garrison going so far as to accuse Douglass of breaking up his own family when an English abolitionist named Julia Griffiths lived with Anna and Frederick Douglass from 1849–1855; there is no evidence she and Douglass were lovers.

melted to tears by his pathos, or roused to virtuous indignation by his stirring eloquence against the enslavers of men!—fortunate for himself, as it at once brought him into the field of public usefulness, "gave the world assurance of a MAN,"[4] quickened the slumbering energies of his soul, and consecrated him to the great work of breaking the rod of the oppressor, and letting the oppressed go free!

I shall never forget his first speech at the convention—the extraordinary emotion it excited in my own mind—the powerful impression it created upon a crowded auditory, completely taken by surprise—the applause which followed from the beginning to the end of his felicitous remarks. I think I never hated slavery so intensely as at that moment; certainly, my perception of the enormous outrage which is inflicted by it, on the godlike nature of its victims, was rendered far more clear than ever. There stood one, in physical proportion and stature commanding and exact—in intellect richly endowed—in natural eloquence a prodigy—in soul manifestly "created but a little lower than the angels"[5]—yet a slave, ay, a fugitive slave,—trembling for his safety, hardly daring to believe that on the American soil, a single white person could be found who would befriend him at all hazards, for the love of God and humanity! Capable of high attainments as an intellectual and moral being—needing nothing but a comparatively small amount of cultivation to make him an ornament to society and a blessing to his race[6]—by the law of the land, by the voice of the people, by the terms of the slave code, he was only a piece of property, a beast of burden, a chattel personal,[7] nevertheless!

A beloved friend[8] from New Bedford prevailed on *Mr. Douglass* to address the convention: He came forward to the platform with a hesitancy

---

4. *Hamlet*, III, iv, 62. In this line Hamlet is explaining to his mother, Queen Gertrude, that her first husband was unquestionably a man, a concept of central concern to Douglass, whose only known work of prose fiction, *The Heroic Slave*, was published in 1852: in the latter work, the full title of which (*The Heroic Slave, a Heartwarming Narrative of the Adventures of Madison Washington, in Pursuit of Liberty*), clearly recalls the title of Douglass's 1845 *Narrative*, Douglass was inspired by the historical Madison Washington, who in 1839 led the most successful slave revolt in United States history against the white crew of a slave ship called the *Creole*. The novel anticipates African Americans fighting for their freedom in the Civil War; in other words, they acted like men.

5. Psalms 8:5; Hebrews 2:7, 9.

6. Compare the still somewhat current term "a credit to his race," which suggests such a black person might almost be white, that is, a human being, in the minds of nineteenth-century white Americans.

7. The idea of humans as personal property was in dispute in the nineteenth century: in England servants were not owned by their masters, as slaves were in the South.

8. Douglass mentions this friend by name in chapter XI as William C. Coffin; he was an abolitionist and friend of Garrison's.

and embarrassment, necessarily the attendants of a sensitive mind in such a novel position. After apologizing for his ignorance,[9] and reminding the audience that slavery was a poor school for the human intellect and heart, he proceeded to narrate some of the facts in his own history as a slave, and in the course of his speech gave utterance to many noble thoughts and thrilling reflections. As soon as he had taken his seat, filled with hope and admiration, I rose, and declared that *Patrick Henry*,[10] of revolutionary fame, never made a speech more eloquent in the cause of liberty, than the one we had just listened to from the lips of that hunted fugitive. So I believed at that time—such is my belief now. I reminded the audience of the peril which surrounded this self-emancipated young man at the North,—even in Massachusetts, on the soil of the Pilgrim Fathers, among the descendants of revolutionary sires; and I appealed to them, whether they would ever allow him to be carried back into slavery,—law or no law, constitution or no constitution. The response was unanimous and in thunder-tones—"NO!" "Will you succor and protect him as a brother-man—resident of the old Bay State?" "YES!" shouted the whole mass, with an energy so startling, that the ruthless tyrants south of Mason and Dixon's line[11] might almost have heard the mighty burst of feeling, and recognized it as the pledge of an invincible determination, on the part of those who gave it, never to betray him that wanders, but to hide the outcast, and firmly to abide the consequences.

It was at once deeply impressed upon my mind, that, if *Mr. Douglass* could be persuaded to consecrate his time and talents to the promotion of the anti-slavery enterprise, a powerful impetus would be given to it, and a stunning blow at the same time inflicted on northern prejudice against a colored complexion. I therefore endeavored to instill hope and courage into his mind, in order that he might dare to engage in a vocation so anomalous and responsible for a person in his situation; and I was seconded in this effort by warm-hearted friends, especially by the late General Agent of the Massachusetts Anti-Slavery Society, *Mr. John A. Collins*, whose judgment in this instance entirely coincided with my own. At first, he could give no encouragement; with unfeigned diffidence, he expressed his conviction that he was not adequate to the performance of so great a task; the path marked out was wholly an untrodden one; he was sincerely apprehensive that he

---

9. Garrison takes Douglass's profession of ignorance as a way of pointing out, as the rest of the sentence implies, that he had been denied an education under slavery.

10. Garrison does not point out that Patrick Henry was a white slaveholder, but Douglass notes the difference in Chapter X: "with us [fugitive slaves] it was a doubtful liberty at most, and almost certain death if we failed. For my [Douglass's] part, I should prefer death to hopeless bondage."

11. The border between the North and the South.

should do more harm than good. After much deliberation, however, he consented to make a trial; and ever since that period, he has acted as a lecturing agent, under the auspices either of the American or the Massachusetts Anti-Slavery Society. In labors he has been most abundant; and his success in combating prejudice, in gaining proselytes, in agitating the public mind, has far surpassed the most sanguine expectations that were raised at the commencement of his brilliant career. He has borne himself with gentleness and meekness, yet with true manliness of character. As a public speaker, he excels in pathos, wit, comparison, imitation, strength of reasoning, and fluency of language. There is in him that union of head and heart, which is indispensable to an enlightenment of the heads and a winning of the hearts of others. May his strength continue to be equal to his day! May he continue to "grow in grace, and in the knowledge of God," that he may be increasingly serviceable in the cause of bleeding humanity, whether at home or abroad!

It is certainly a very remarkable fact, that one of the most efficient advocates of the slave population, now before the public, is a fugitive slave, in the person of *Frederick Douglass*; and that the free colored population of the United States are as ably represented by one of their own number, in the person of *Charles Lenox Remond*,[12] whose eloquent appeals have extorted the highest applause of multitudes on both sides of the Atlantic. Let the calumniators of the colored race despise themselves for their baseness and illiberality of spirit, and henceforth cease to talk of the natural inferiority of those who require nothing but time and opportunity to attain to the highest point of human excellence.

It may, perhaps, be fairly questioned, whether any other portion of the population of the earth could have endured the privations, sufferings and horrors of slavery, without having become more degraded in the scale of humanity than the slaves of African descent. Nothing has been left undone to cripple their intellects, darken their minds, debase their moral nature, obliterate all traces of their relationship to mankind; and yet how wonderfully they have sustained the mighty load of a most frightful bondage, under which they have been groaning for centuries! To illustrate the effect of slavery on the white man,—to show that he has no powers of endurance, in such a condition, superior to those of his black brother,—*Daniel O'Connell*,[13] the distinguished advocate of universal emancipation, and the

---

12. He and Douglass worked for the Massachusetts Anti-Slavery Society as lecturers on abolition (Reverend Remond was also black).

13. The Irish patriot whom Douglass greatly admired; Douglass was struck by the parallel between the Irish and the English, and slaves and slaveowners.

mightiest champion of prostrate but not conquered Ireland, relates the following anecdote in a speech delivered by him in the Conciliation Hall, Dublin, before the Loyal National Repeal Association, March 31, 1845. "No matter," said Mr. O'connell, "under what specious term it may disguise itself, slavery is still hideous. *It has a natural, an inevitable tendency to brutalize every noble faculty of man.* An American sailor, who was cast away on the shore of Africa, where he was kept in slavery for three years, was, at the expiration of that period, found to be imbruted and stultified— he had lost all reasoning power; and having forgotten his native language, could only utter some savage gibberish between Arabic and English, which nobody could understand, and which even he himself found difficulty in pronouncing. So much for the humanizing influence of *The Domestic Institution!*" Admitting this to have been an extraordinary case of mental deterioration, it proves at least that the white slave can sink as low in the scale of humanity as the black one.

Mr. Douglass has very properly chosen to write his own Narrative, in his own style, and according to the best of his ability, rather than to employ some one else. It is, therefore, entirely his own production; and, considering how long and dark was the career he had to run as a slave,—how few have been his opportunities to improve his mind since he broke his iron fetters,—it is, in my judgment, highly creditable to his head and heart. He who can peruse it without a tearful eye, a heaving breast, an afflicted spirit,—without being filled with an unutterable abhorrence of slavery and all its abettors, and animated with a determination to seek the immediate overthrow of that execrable system,—without trembling for the fate of this country in the hands of a righteous God, who is ever on the side of the oppressed, and whose arm is not shortened that it cannot save,—must have a flinty heart, and be qualified to act the part of a trafficker "in slaves and the souls of men."[14] I am confident that it is essentially true in all its statements; that nothing has been set down in malice, nothing exaggerated, nothing drawn from the imagination;[15] that it comes short of the reality, rather than overstates a single fact in regard to slavery as it is. The experience of Frederick Douglass, as a slave, was not a peculiar one; his lot was not especially a hard one; his case may be regarded as a very fair specimen of the treatment of slaves in Maryland, in which State it is conceded that they are better fed and less cruelly treated than in Georgia, Alabama, or Louisiana. Many have suffered incomparably more, while very few on the

---

14. See Revelation 18:13.

15. Actually, Douglass's *Narrative* does omit and alter facts according to Douglass's artistic needs, just as all other autobiographies do.

plantations have suffered less, than himself. Yet how deplorable was his situation! what terrible chastisements were inflicted upon his person! what still more shocking outrages were perpetrated upon his mind! with all his noble powers and sublime aspirations, how like a brute was he treated, even by those professing to have the same mind in them that was in Christ Jesus! to what dreadful liabilities was he continually subjected! how destitute of friendly counsel and aid, even in his greatest extremities! how heavy was the midnight of woe which shrouded in blackness the last ray of hope, and filled the future with terror and gloom! what longings after freedom took possession of his breast, and how his misery augmented, in proportion as he grew reflective and intelligent,—thus demonstrating that a happy slave is an extinct man! how he thought, reasoned, felt, under the lash of the driver, with the chains upon his limbs! what perils he encountered in his endeavors to escape from his horrible doom! and how signal have been his deliverance and preservation in the midst of a nation of pitiless enemies!

This Narrative contains many affecting incidents, many passages of great eloquence and power; but I think the most thrilling one of them all is the description *Douglass* gives of his feelings, as he stood soliloquizing respecting his fate, and the chances of his one day being a freeman, on the banks of the Chesapeake Bay—viewing the receding vessels as they flew with their white wings before the breeze, and apostrophizing them as animated by the living spirit of freedom. Who can read that passage, and be insensible to its pathos and sublimity? Compressed into it is a whole Alexandrian library[16] of thought, feeling, and sentiment—all that can, all that need be urged, in the form of expostulation, entreaty, rebuke, against that crime of crimes,—making man the property of his fellow-man! O, how accursed is that system, which entombs the godlike mind of man, defaces the divine image, reduces those who by creation were crowned with glory and honor to a level with four-footed beasts, and exalts the dealer in human flesh above all that is called God! Why should its existence be prolonged one hour? Is it not evil, only evil, and that continually? What does its presence imply but the absence of all fear of God, all regard for man, on the part of the people of the United States? Heaven speed its eternal overthrow!

So profoundly ignorant of the nature of slavery are many persons, that they are stubbornly incredulous whenever they read or listen to any recital of the cruelties which are daily inflicted on its victims. They do not deny

---

16. Famous library in Egypt that contained many of the masterpieces of ancient Greece and Rome.

that the slaves are held as property; but that terrible fact seems to convey to their minds no idea of injustice, exposure to outrage, or savage barbarity. Tell them of cruel scourgings, of mutilations and brandings, of scenes of pollution and blood, of the banishment of all light and knowledge, and they affect to be greatly indignant at such enormous exaggerations, such whole-sale misstatements, such abominable libels on the character of the southern planters! As if all these direful outrages were not the natural results of slavery! As if it were less cruel to reduce a human being to the condition of a thing, than to give him a severe flagellation, or to deprive him of necessary food and clothing! As if whips, chains, thumb-screws, paddles, blood-hounds, overseers, drivers, patrols,[17] were not all indispensable to keep the slaves down, and to give protection to their ruthless oppressors! As if, when the marriage institution is abolished,[18] concubinage, adultery, and incest, must not necessarily abound; when all the rights of humanity are annihilated, any barrier remains to protect the victim from the fury of the spoiler; when absolute power is assumed over life and liberty, it will not be wielded with destructive sway! Skeptics of this character abound in society. In some few instances, their incredulity arises from a want of reflection; but, generally, it indicates a hatred of the light, a desire to shield slavery from the assaults of its foes, a contempt of the colored race, whether bond or free. Such will try to discredit the shocking tales of slaveholding cruelty which are recorded in this truthful Narrative; but they will labor in vain. *Mr. Douglass* has frankly disclosed the place of his birth, the names of those who claimed ownership in his body and soul, and

---

17. Patrols comprised of armed white males were allowed to enter the slave quarters to search for weapons and ammunition that could be used in slave insurrections. It is this tradition that some historians relate to some fatal shootings of black men by the police in American cities today and behind the bad relations in general between the police and African Americans now. See Sally E. Haddon, *Slave Patrols* (Cambridge, MA: Harvard University Press, 2001).

18. Slave marriages had no legal sanction, which is why Douglass reproduces his marriage certificate for his first wife in his narrative. He wanted readers to know their marriage was legal and that she was not an opportunity for any white male sexual predator. Many nineteenth-century whites, mistaking the silence of sexually exploited female slaves as assent, thought the latter were unrapeable, that is, they were like animals in heat when it came to white men. Even where longstanding relationships between black couples were recognized as the equivalent of legally married after the Civil War, the word did not reach remote areas of the South until years after the war, which left former slave women at the mercy of white men. The effect of white male sexual license on white families was also devastating, as Harriet Jacobs makes painfully clear in her *Incidents in the Life of a Slave Girl* (1861), a slave narrative written from a black woman's point of view.

the names also of those who committed the crimes which he has alleged against them. His statements, therefore, may easily be disproved, if they are untrue.[19]

In the course of his Narrative, he relates two instances of murderous cruelty,—in one of which a planter deliberately shot a slave belonging to a neighboring plantation, who had unintentionally gotten within his lordly domain in quest of fish; and in the other, an overseer blew out the brains of a slave who had fled to a stream of water to escape a bloody scourging. *Mr. Douglass* states that in neither of these instances was any thing done by way of legal arrest or judicial investigation. The Baltimore American, of March 17, 1845, relates a similar case of atrocity, perpetrated with similar impunity—as follows:—"*Shooting a slave.*—We learn, upon the authority of a letter from Charles county, Maryland, received by a gentleman of this city, that a young man, named Matthews, a nephew of General Matthews, and whose father, it is believed, holds an office at Washington, killed one of the slaves upon his father's farm by shooting him. The letter states that young Matthews had been left in charge of the farm; that he gave an order to the servant, which was disobeyed, when he proceeded to the house, *obtained a gun, and, returning, shot the servant.* He immediately, the letter continues, fled to his father's residence, where he still remains unmolested."—Let it never be forgotten, that no slaveholder or overseer can be convicted of any outrage perpetrated on the person of a slave, however diabolical it may be, on the testimony of colored witnesses, whether bond or free. By the slave code, they are adjudged to be as incompetent to testify against a white man, as though they were indeed a part of the brute creation. Hence, there is no legal protection in fact, whatever there may be in form, for the slave population; and any amount of cruelty may be inflicted on them with impunity. Is it possible for the human mind to conceive of a more horrible state of society?

The effect of a religious profession on the conduct of southern masters is vividly described in the following Narrative, and shown to be any thing but salutary. In the nature of the case, it must be in the highest degree pernicious. The testimony of *Mr. Douglass*, on this point, is sustained by a cloud of witnesses, whose veracity is unimpeachable. "A slaveholder's profession of Christianity is a palpable imposture. He is a felon of the highest grade. He is a man-stealer. It is of no importance what you put in the other scale."

Reader! are you with the man-stealers in sympathy and purpose, or on the side of their down-trodden victims? If with the former, then are you the

---

19. White southerners who wrote attacks on Douglass's *Narrative* inadvertently proved he was telling the truth by mentioning the same names, dates, and places Douglass mentions.

foe of God and man. If with the latter, what are you prepared to do and dare in their behalf? Be faithful, be vigilant, be untiring in your efforts to break every yoke, and let the oppressed go free. Come what may— cost what it may—inscribe on the banner which you unfurl to the breeze, as your religious and political motto—"NO COMPROMISE WITH SLAVERY! NO UNION WITH SLAVEHOLDERS!"[20]
WM. LLOYD GARRISON BOSTON,
May 1, 1845.

LETTER FROM WENDELL PHILLIPS, ESQ.[21]
BOSTON, APRIL 22, 1845.

My Dear Friend:
You remember the old fable of "The Man and the Lion," where the lion complained that he should not be so misrepresented "when the lions wrote history."

I am glad the time has come when the "lions write history." We have been left long enough to gather the character of slavery from the involuntary evidence of the masters. One might, indeed, rest sufficiently satisfied with what, it is evident, must be, in general, the results of such a relation, without seeking farther to find whether they have followed in every instance. Indeed, those who stare at the half-peck of corn a week, and love to count the lashes on the slave's back, are seldom the "stuff" out of which reformers and abolitionists are to be made. I remember that, in 1838, many were waiting for the results of the West India experiment, before they could come into our ranks. Those "results" have come long ago; but, alas! few of that number have come with them, as converts. A man must be disposed to judge of emancipation by other tests than whether it has increased the produce of sugar,—and to hate slavery for other reasons than

---

20. Garrison wanted the North to secede from the Union, which might have been a catastrophe for the slaves, but if the North had seceded, Lincoln would not have had to worry about protecting the Constitutional rights of slaveholders to own slaves because the federal Constitution would not have applied to a south that was not part of the Union as a result of the North leaving it. Garrison also advocated northern secession because he thought the Union would then be a haven for escaped slaves, there would be diminished government support for quelling slave insurrections, and diminished slave-state claims on new territories. See Henry Mayer, *All on Fire: William Lloyd Garrison and the Abolition of Slavery* (New York: St. Martin's Press, 1998), p. 452. The opposing argument was that northern secession would have preserved slavery, presumably by allowing the slave states to set up a more comprehensive police state of their own. In 1845, Douglass agreed that the North should secede.

21. Like Garrison, Wendell Phillips was one of the leading white abolitionists; he, too, wanted the North to secede from the Union, which might or might not have ended slavery.

because it starves men and whips women,—before he is ready to lay the first stone of his anti-slavery life.

I was glad to learn, in your story, how early the most neglected of God's children waken to a sense of their rights, and of the injustice done them. Experience is a keen teacher; and long before you had mastered your A B C, or knew where the "white sails" of the Chesapeake were bound, you began, I see, to gauge the wretchedness of the slave, not by his hunger and want, not by his lashes and toil, but by the cruel and blighting death which gathers over his soul.[22]

In connection with this, there is one circumstance which makes your recollections peculiarly valuable, and renders your early insight the more remarkable. You come from that part of the country where we are told slavery appears with its fairest features. Let us hear, then, what it is at its best estate—gaze on its bright side, if it has one; and then imagination may task her powers to add dark lines to the picture, as she travels southward to that (for the colored man) Valley of the Shadow of Death,[23] where the Mississippi sweeps along.

Again, we have known you long, and can put the most entire confidence in your truth, candor, and sincerity. Every one who has heard you speak has felt, and, I am confident, every one who reads your book will feel, persuaded that you give them a fair specimen of the whole truth. No one-sided portrait,—no wholesale complaints,—but strict justice done, whenever individual kindliness has neutralized, for a moment, the deadly system with which it was strangely allied. You have been with us, too, some years, and can fairly compare the twilight of rights, which your race enjoy at the North, with that "noon of night" under which they labor south of Mason and Dixon's line. Tell us whether, after all, the half-free colored man of Massachusetts is worse off than the pampered slave of the rice swamps!

In reading your life, no one can say that we have unfairly picked out some rare specimens of cruelty. We know that the bitter drops, which even you have drained from the cup, are no incidental aggravations, no individual ills, but such as must mingle always and necessarily in the lot of every slave. They are the essential ingredients, not the occasional results, of the system.

After all, I shall read your book with trembling for you. Some years ago, when you were beginning to tell me your real name and birthplace, you may remember I stopped you, and preferred to remain ignorant of all. With the exception of a vague description, so I continued, till the other

---

22. In 1901, W. E. B. Du Bois in *The Souls of Black Folk* also imagined African American life as a living death.
23. Psalms 23:4.

day, when you read me your memoirs. I hardly knew, at the time, whether to thank you or not for the sight of them, when I reflected that it was still dangerous, in Massachusetts, for honest men to tell their names! They say the fathers, in 1776, signed the Declaration of Independence with the halter about their necks. You, too, publish your declaration of freedom with danger compassing you around. In all the broad lands which the Constitution of the United States overshadows, there is no single spot,—however narrow or desolate,—where a fugitive slave can plant himself and say, "I am safe." The whole armory of Northern Law has no shield for you. I am free to say that, in your place, I should throw the MS. into the fire.

You, perhaps, may tell your story in safety, endeared as you are to so many warm hearts by rare gifts, and a still rarer devotion of them to the service of others. But it will be owing only to your labors, and the fearless efforts of those who, trampling the laws and Constitution[24] of the country under their feet, are determined that they will "hide the outcast," and that their hearths shall be, spite of the law, an asylum for the oppressed, if, some time or other, the humblest may stand in our streets, and bear witness in safety against the cruelties of which he has been the victim.

Yet it is sad to think, that these very throbbing hearts which welcome your story, and form your best safeguard in telling it, are all beating contrary to the "statute in such case made and provided."[25] Go on, my dear friend, till you, and those who, like you, have been saved, so as by fire, from the dark prison-house, shall stereotype these free, illegal pulses into statutes; and New England, cutting loose from a blood-stained Union, shall glory in being the house of refuge for the oppressed,—till we no longer merely "hide the outcast,"[26] or make a merit of standing idly by while he is hunted in our midst; but, consecrating anew the soil of the Pilgrims as an asylum for the oppressed, proclaim our *welcome* to the slave

---

24. There was substantial argument in the nineteenth century over the question of whether the Constitution supported slavery. When Douglass published the *Narrative* in 1845, he agreed with Phillips and Garrison that the Constitution supported it, but later he reversed course and argued that it did not. Douglass had a flexible intellect that was ultimately presided over by general principles rather than purity about avoiding contradiction. To him the abolition of slavery mattered more than consistency in his interpretation of the Constitution.

25. A wordy yet precise way of referring to a particular law, when charging someone with breaking it. Phillips seems to be referring to the Fugitive Slave Act of 1793. His quotation marks around that phrase indicated that it was commonly used as a rhetorical sleight of hand, as that dull phrase masks a law with a vivid, monstrous name, "Fugitive Slave Act." Confer also "peculiar institution" for slavery.

26. Isaiah 16:3.

CHAPTER I

I was born in Tuckahoe, near Hillsborough, and about twelve miles from Easton, in Talbot County, Maryland. I have no accurate knowledge of my age, never having seen any authentic record containing it.[27] By far the larger part of the slaves know as little of their ages as horses know of theirs, and it is the wish of most masters within my knowledge to keep their slaves thus ignorant. I do not remember to have ever met a slave who could tell of his birthday. They seldom come nearer to it than planting-time, harvest-time, cherry-time, spring-time, or fall-time. A want of information concerning my own was a source of unhappiness to me even during childhood. The white children could tell their ages. I could not tell why I ought to be deprived of the same privilege. I was not allowed to make any inquiries of my master concerning it. He deemed all such inquiries on the part of a slave improper and impertinent, and evidence of a restless spirit. The nearest estimate I can give makes me now between twenty-seven and twenty-eight years of age. I come to this, from hearing my master say, some time during 1835, I was about seventeen years old.[28]

---

27. Denying slaves such basic autobiographical knowledge indicates their status is like that of a cow or a horse; we now know that Douglass was born in February, 1818.
28. It is brightly revealing to put Douglass's first paragraph next to Booker T. Washington's in *Up from Slavery* (1901):

> "I WAS born a slave on a plantation in Franklin County, Virginia. I am not quite sure of the exact place or exact date of my birth, but at any rate I suspect I must have been born somewhere and at some time. As nearly as I have been able to learn, I was born near a crossroads post-office called Hale's Ford, and the year was 1858 or 1859. I do not know the month or the day. The earliest impressions I can now recall are of the plantation and the slave quarters—the latter being the part of the plantation where the slaves had their cabins."

Clearly, Washington plays dumb to win white financial support for Tuskegee Institute, as it was then called. Using the syntax and vocabulary of an elementary school primer, so as not to seem "uppity," Washington contends that he must have been born someplace and sometime, an intentionally self-deprecating statement to bolster the white reader's smug sense of "superiority," but this strategy worked: Washington's pose got moneyed whites to support him; he had lunch with President Theodore Roosevelt in the White House; he reassured whites elsewhere in *Up from Slavery* that blacks should wait to get the vote. Douglass is more straightforward and literary in style, but his audience was northern white liberals. The mistake many white readers made about Washington's apparent simple-mindedness was to confuse his means with his ends. In other words, if writing paragraphs of inert prose would get a black person's foot on the first rung of the social ladder, which could then be climbed, Washington was willing to write them. Douglass was more concerned about dignity for himself and other blacks in 1845, not later. He realized "wait" meant never for African Americans.

My mother was named Harriet Bailey. She was the daughter of Isaac and Betsey Bailey, both colored, and quite dark. My mother was of a darker complexion than either my grandmother or grandfather.

My father was a white man. He was admitted to be such by all I ever heard speak of my parentage. The opinion was also whispered that my master was my father; but of the correctness of this opinion, I know nothing; the means of knowing was withheld from me.[29] My mother and I were separated when I was but an infant—before I knew her as my mother. It is a common custom, in the part of Maryland from which I ran away, to part children from their mothers at a very early age. Frequently, before the child has reached its twelfth month, its mother is taken from it, and hired out on some farm a considerable distance off, and the child is placed under the care of an old woman, too old for field labor. For what this separation is done, I do not know, unless it be to hinder the development of the child's affection toward its mother, and to blunt and destroy the natural affection of the mother for the child. This is the inevitable result.

I never saw my mother, to know her as such, more than four or five times in my life; and each of these times was very short in duration, and at night. She was hired by a Mr. Stewart, who lived about twelve miles from my home.[30] She made her journeys to see me in the night, travelling the whole distance on foot, after the performance of her day's work. She was a field hand, and a whipping is the penalty of not being in the field at sunrise, unless a slave has special permission from his or her master to the contrary—a permission which they seldom get, and one that gives to him that gives it the

---

29. Again, the appalling arrogance of a system that would conceal such vital information from a child is hard for modern readers to understand: the message is that slaves do not matter any more than a donkey does. It is quite possible that Aaron Anthony was Douglass's father (Dickson J. Preston, *Young Frederick Douglass*, p. 22). Whoever he was, Douglass's father was not under any strong ethical requirement or social custom that he would publically acknowledge his son, nor would the charge of rape, if that is what occurred, have been likely because black women were not considered rapeable, since they were considered to be sexual animals by whites. If the relationship between Douglass's parents had any love in it that is unlikely to have been revealed.

30. Actually, as Douglass acknowledged in *My Bondage and My Freedom*, it was not until Douglass was six years old that she had to walk twelve miles to see him, but in the 1845 *Narrative*, this gave the false impression that when he was an infant his mother was sent to work twelve miles away while he was placed under the care of his grandmother.

In fact, this was not the case at all, and Douglass tried to correct the record in *My Bondage and My Freedom*. There he made it clear that it was not until after he moved to the Lloyd plantation at the age of six that his mother had to travel twelve miles to visit him. The twelve miles was from the Tuckahoe Creek farm to Wye House, not from Stewart's farm to Tuckahoe Creek. Nevertheless, the notion that his mother was sent away when he was but an infant, so that they could not see each other, remains firmly fixed as part of the Douglass myth (Preston, p. 219, note 9).

proud name of being a kind master. I do not recollect of ever seeing my mother by the light of day. She was with me in the night. She would lie down with me, and get me to sleep, but long before I waked she was gone. Very little communication ever took place between us. Death soon ended what little we could have while she lived, and with it her hardships and suffering. She died when I was about seven years old, on one of my master's farms, near Lee's Mill. I was not allowed to be present during her illness, at her death, or burial. She was gone long before I knew any thing about it. Never having enjoyed, to any considerable extent, her soothing presence, her tender and watchful care, I received the tidings of her death with much the same emotions I should have probably felt at the death of a stranger.

Called thus suddenly away, she left me without the slightest intimation of who my father was. The whisper that my master was my father, may or may not be true; and, true or false, it is of but little consequence to my purpose whilst the fact remains, in all its glaring odiousness, that slaveholders have ordained, and by law established, that the children of slave women shall in all cases follow the condition of their mothers; and this is done too obviously to administer to their own lusts, and make a gratification of their wicked desires profitable as well as pleasurable; for by this cunning arrangement, the slaveholder, in cases not a few, sustains to his slaves the double relation of master and father.

I know of such cases; and it is worthy of remark that such slaves invariably suffer greater hardships, and have more to contend with, than others. They are, in the first place, a constant offence to their mistress. She is ever disposed to find fault with them; they can seldom do any thing to please her; she is never better pleased than when she sees them under the lash, especially when she suspects her husband of showing to his mulatto children favors which he withholds from his black slaves. The master is frequently compelled to sell this class of his slaves, out of deference to the feelings of his white wife; and, cruel as the deed may strike any one to be, for a man to sell his own children to human flesh-mongers, it is often the dictate of humanity for him to do so; for, unless he does this, he must not only whip them himself, but must stand by and see one white son tie up his brother, of but few shades darker complexion than himself, and ply the gory lash to his naked back; and if he lisp one word of disapproval, it is set down to his parental partiality, and only makes a bad matter worse, both for himself and the slave whom he would protect and defend.[31]

---

31. Another effect of white men taking sexual advantage of enslaved black women was the subversion of potential sisterhood between the white wives of the masters and the enslaved black women. Some masters relished being the object of jealousy when their wives learned of their promiscuity with slave mothers. Harriet Jacobs dramatizes an example in *Incidents in the Life of a Slave Girl.*

Every year brings with it multitudes of this class of slaves. It was doubtless in consequence of a knowledge of this fact, that one great statesman of the south predicted the downfall of slavery by the inevitable laws of population. Whether this prophecy is ever fulfilled or not, it is nevertheless plain that a very different-looking class of people are springing up at the south, and are now held in slavery, from those originally brought to this country from Africa; and if their increase do no other good, it will do away the force of the argument, that God cursed Ham,[32] and therefore American slavery is right. If the lineal descendants of Ham are alone to be scripturally enslaved, it is certain that slavery at the south must soon become unscriptural; for thousands are ushered into the world, annually, who, like myself, owe their existence to white fathers, and those fathers most frequently their own masters.

I have had two masters. My first master's name was Anthony. I do not remember his first name. He was generally called Captain Anthony—a title which, I presume, he acquired by sailing a craft on the Chesapeake Bay. He was not considered a rich slaveholder. He owned two or three farms, and about thirty slaves. His farms and slaves were under the care of an overseer. The overseer's name was Plummer. Mr. Plummer was a miserable drunkard, a profane swearer, and a savage monster. He always went armed with a cowskin and a heavy cudgel. I have known him to cut and slash the women's heads so horribly, that even master would be enraged at his cruelty, and would threaten to whip him if he did not mind himself. Master, however, was not a humane slaveholder. It required extraordinary barbarity on the part of an overseer to affect him. He was a cruel man, hardened by a long life of slaveholding. He would at times seem to take great pleasure in whipping a slave. I have often been awakened at the dawn of day by the most heart-rending shrieks of an own aunt of mine, whom he used to tie up to a joist, and whip upon her naked back till she was literally covered with blood. No words, no tears, no prayers, from his gory victim, seemed to move his iron heart from its bloody purpose. The louder she screamed, the harder he whipped; and where the blood ran fastest, there he whipped longest. He would whip her to make her scream, and whip her to make her hush; and not until overcome by fatigue, would he cease to swing the blood-clotted cowskin. I remember the first time I ever witnessed this horrible exhibition. I was quite a child, but I well remember it. I never shall forget it whilst I remember any thing. It was the first of a long series of such outrages, of which I was doomed to be a witness and a participant. It struck me with awful force. It was the blood-stained gate, the entrance to the hell of slavery, through which I was about to pass. It

---

32. See Genesis 9:20–27, for the source of the preposterous argument that the descendants of Noah's son Ham were cursed by God to servitude.

was a most terrible spectacle. I wish I could commit to paper the feelings with which I beheld it.

This occurrence took place very soon after I went to live with my old master, and under the following circumstances. Aunt Hester went out one night,—where or for what I do not know,—and happened to be absent when my master desired her presence. He had ordered her not to go out evenings, and warned her that she must never let him catch her in company with a young man, who was paying attention to her belonging to Colonel Lloyd. The young man's name was Ned Roberts, generally called Lloyd's Ned. Why master was so careful of her, may be safely left to conjecture. She was a woman of noble form, and of graceful proportions, having very few equals, and fewer superiors, in personal appearance, among the colored or white women of our neighborhood.

Aunt Hester had not only disobeyed his orders in going out, but had been found in company with Lloyd's Ned; which circumstance, I found, from what he said while whipping her, was the chief offence. Had he been a man of pure morals himself, he might have been thought interested in protecting the innocence of my aunt; but those who knew him will not suspect him of any such virtue. Before he commenced whipping Aunt Hester, he took her into the kitchen, and stripped her from neck to waist, leaving her neck, shoulders, and back, entirely naked. He then told her to cross her hands, calling her at the same time a d——b b——h.[33] After crossing her hands, he tied them with a strong rope, and led her to a stool under a large hook in the joist, put in for the purpose. He made her get upon the stool, and tied her hands to the hook. She now stood fair for his infernal purpose. Her arms were stretched up at their full length, so that she stood upon the ends of her toes. He then said to her, "Now, you d——b b——h, I'll learn you how to disobey my orders!" and after rolling up his sleeves, he commenced to lay on the heavy cowskin, and soon the warm, red blood

---

33. An example of nineteenth-century gentility, "d——b," for "damn bitch," may seem hypocritical or prudish to contemporary readers, but it indicates Douglass's gentility in a century when women seldom perspired or demanded sexual fulfillment in American literature; readers of *The Scarlet Letter*, published five years after Douglass's *Narrative*, were shocked that Hester Prynne had not been struck by lightning for committing adultery. The knees of piano legs were covered, gentlemen did not remove their coats while ladies were present, and one did not ask for a breast of chicken at the dinner table. It is in Douglass's interest to present himself to readers as a gentleman according to standards prevailing in 1845, when his *Narrative* was published. It should also be noted here that Douglass may tend to represent black women as passive victims, black men as agents. Along with Herman Melville, Douglass chafed at the hypocrisy of having to censor language and events, while both went uncensored in real life; descriptions of the whipping and raping of black women were "genteel," while of course in reality such activities were anything but refined.

(amid heart-rending shrieks from her, and horrid oaths from him) came dripping to the floor. I was so terrified and horror-stricken at the sight, that I hid myself in a closet, and dared not venture out till long after the bloody transaction was over. I expected it would be my turn next.[34] It was all new to me. I had never seen any thing like it before. I had always lived with my grandmother on the outskirts of the plantation, where she was put to raise the children of the younger women. I had therefore been, until now, out of the way of the bloody scenes that often occurred on the plantation.[35]

---

34. As David Van Leer points out in his essay in *Frederick Douglass & Herman Melville: Essays in Relation* (pp. 279–299), on the one hand, this sentence could mean Douglass thought he might be whipped next; on the other hand, it could mean he himself would whip Hester next. In other words, Douglass may identify with Anthony rather than Hester, an extremely unsettling possibility to Douglass. It is even possible that Anthony could have forced Douglass to rape Hester or that Anthony could have raped Douglass.

35. When Douglass wrote his autobiography again, published in 1855 and entitled *My Bondage and My Freedom*, he included a passage on his boyhood from quite a different perspective from the one he adopted in the *Narrative*:

"The slaveholder, having nothing to fear from impotent childhood, easily affords to refrain from cruel inflictions; and if cold and hunger do not pierce the tender frame, the first seven or eight years of the slave-boy's life are about as full of sweet content as those of the most favored and petted white children of the slaveholder. The slave-boy escapes many troubles which befall and vex his white brother. He seldom has to listen to lectures on propriety of behavior, or on anything else. He is never chided for handling his little knife and fork improperly or awkwardly, for he uses none. He is never reprimanded for soiling the table-cloth, for he takes his meals on the clay floor. He never has the misfortune, in his games or sports, of soiling or tearing his clothes, for he has almost none to soil or tear. He is never expected to act like a nice little gentleman, for he is only a rude little slave. Thus, freed from all restraint, the slave-boy can be, in his life and conduct, a genuine boy, doing whatever his boyish nature suggests; enacting, by turns, all the strange antics and freaks of horses, dogs, pigs, and barn-door fowls, without in any manner compromising his dignity, or incurring reproach of any sort. He literally runs wild; has no pretty little verses to learn in the nursery; no nice little speeches to make for aunts, uncles, or cousins, to show how smart he is; and, if he can only manage to keep out of the way of the heavy feet and fists of the older slave boys, he may trot on, in his joyous and roguish tricks, as happy as any little heathen under the palm trees of Africa. To be sure, he is occasionally reminded, when he stumbles in the path of his master—and this he early learns to avoid—that he is eating his 'white bread,' and that he will be made to 'see sights' by-and-by. The threat is soon forgotten; the shadow soon passes, and our sable boy continues to roll in the dust, or play in the mud, as bests suits him, and in the veriest freedom. If he feels uncomfortable, from mud or from dust, the coast is clear; he can plunge into the river or the pond, without the ceremony of undressing, or the fear of wetting his clothes; his little tow-linen shirt—for that is all he has on—is easily dried; and it needed ablution as much as did his skin. His food is of the coarsest kind, consisting for the most part of cornmeal mush, which often finds it way from the wooden tray to his mouth in an oyster shell. His days, when the weather is warm, are spent in the pure, open air, and in the bright sunshine. He always sleeps in airy apartments; he seldom has to take powders, or to be paid to swallow pretty little sugar-coated pills, to cleanse his blood, or to quicken his appetite. He eats no candies; gets no lumps of loaf sugar; always relishes his food; cries but little, for nobody cares for his crying; learns to esteem his bruises but slight, because others so esteem them. In a word, he is, for the most part of the first eight years of his life, a spirited, joyous, uproarious, and happy boy, upon whom troubles fall only like water on a duck's back. And such a boy, so far as I can now remember, was the boy whose life in slavery I am now narrating." (*My Bondage and My Freedom*. New York and Auburn: Miller, Orton, & Mulligan, 1855.)

This passage indicate that Douglass's boyhood may not have been as dark as the *Narrative* suggested it was. Has Douglass mellowed, has his memory betrayed him, has he reconsidered his earlier impression of his early life? These fascinating questions, and there are numerous other possibilities, along with another problem, greatly complicate our interpretation of his boyhood in his first two versions of his life; the other problem is that, as is the case with any first-person autobiography, there are three versions of the author, in this case Frederick Douglasses: the historical person, the narrator, and the character. If the distinctions are not maintained, Douglass may have lost control of his readers' responses to his text. If the historical Douglass lets his narrator look back at his younger self with nostalgia, for example, ten years after he and his narrator first looked back at him, he may have represented his boyhood more self-indulgently than he did in the *Narrative*. Whatever the case, many readers will find the second version of his boyhood a challenge to his first. When writers allow the distinction between themselves as historical personages, as narrators, and as characters to collapse, they create intriguing interpretive problems for their readers. It could also be the case that Douglass was being sarcastic in his 1855 characterization of his boyhood.

Over forty years later, Douglass would give a speech in Washington, D.C., in which he depicted women as active agents of their right to vote, but few contemporary readers are familiar with it, which helps explain why so many have a frozen concept of Douglass's view of women as passive victims of male power and authority. But Douglass had an unusually active mind and was comfortable with the principle of falsifiability: the notion that people should be able to tell intellectual opponents what would change their minds. Douglass always stood ready to modify his views when he was presented with compelling counter-evidence to his ideas. Consequently, after he witnessed over forty years worth of evidence that women, black and nonblack, could resist male power, he changed his mind. The risk he took was that some viewed his willingness to change as a weakness or an irritation. The speech is as follows:

"Mrs. President, Ladies and Gentlemen:—I come to this platform with unusual diffidence. Although I have long been identified with the Woman's Suffrage movement, and have often spoken in its favor, I am somewhat at a loss to know what to say on this really great and uncommon occasion, where so much has been said.

"When I look around on this assembly, and see the many able and eloquent women, full of the subject, ready to speak, and who only need the opportunity to impress this audience with their views and thrill them with "thoughts that breathe and words that burn," I do not feel like taking up more than a very small space of your time and attention, and shall not. I would not, even now, presume to speak, but for the circumstance of my early connection with the cause, and of having been called upon to do so by one whose voice in this Council we all gladly obey. Men have very little business here as speakers, anyhow; and if they come here at all they should take back benches and wrap themselves in silence. For this is an International Council, not of men, but of women, and woman should have all the say in it. This is her day in court. I do not mean to exalt the intellect of woman above man's; but I have heard many men speak on this subject, some of them the most eloquent to be found anywhere in the country; and I believe no man, however gifted with thought and speech, can voice the wrongs and present the demands of women with the skill and effect, with the power and authority of woman herself. The man struck is the man to cry out. Woman knows and feels her wrongs as man cannot know and feel them, and she also knows as well as he can know, what measures are needed to redress them. I grant all the claims at this point.

She is her own best representative. We can neither speak for her, nor vote for her, nor act for her, nor be responsible for her; and the thing for men to do in the premises is just to get out of her way and give her the fullest opportunity to exercise all the powers inherent in her individual personality, and allow her to do it as she herself shall elect to exercise them. Her right to be and to do is as full, complete and perfect as the right of any man on earth. I say of her, as I say of the colored people, 'Give her fair play, and hands off.' There was a time when, perhaps, we men could help a little. It was when this woman suffrage cause was in its cradle, when it was not big enough to go alone, when it had to be taken in the arms of its mother from Seneca Falls, N.Y., to Rochester, N.Y., for baptism. I then went along with it and offered my services to help it, for then it needed help; but now it can afford to dispense with me and all of my sex. Then its friends were few—now its friends are many. Then it was wrapped in obscurity—now it is lifted in sight of the whole civilized world, and people of all lands and languages give it their hearty support. Truly the change is vast and wonderful.

"I thought my eye of faith was tolerably clear when I attended those meetings in Seneca Falls and Rochester, but it was far too dim to see at the end of forty years a result so imposing as this International Council, and to see yourself [Elizabeth Cady Stanton] and Miss Anthony alive and active in its proceedings. Of course, I expected to be alive myself, and am not surprised to find myself so; for such is, perhaps, the presumption and arrogance common to my sex. Nevertheless, I am very glad to see you here to-day, and to see this great assembly of women. I am glad that you are its president. No manufactured 'boom,' or political contrivance, such as make presidents elsewhere, has made you president of this assembly of women in this Capital of the Nation. You hold your place by reason of eminent fitness, and I give you joy that your life and labors in the cause of woman are thus crowned with honor and glory. This I say in spite of the warning given us by Miss Anthony's friend against mutual admiration.

"There may be some well-meaning people in this audience who have never attended a woman suffrage convention, never heard a woman suffrage speech, never read a woman suffrage newspaper, and they may be surprised that those who speak here do not argue the question. It may be kind to tell them that our cause has passed beyond the period of arguing. The demand of the hour is not argument, but assertion, firm and inflexible assertion, assertion which has more than the force of an argument. If there is any argument to be made, it must be made by opponents, not by the friends of woman suffrage. Let those who want argument examine the ground upon which they base their claim to the right to vote. They will find that there is not one reason, not one consideration, which they can urge in support of man's claim to vote, which does not equally support the right of woman to vote.

"There is to-day, however, a special reason for omitting argument. This is the end of the fought decade of the woman suffrage movement, a kind of jubilee which naturally turns our minds to the past.

"Ever since this Council has been in session, my thoughts have been reverting to the past. I have been thinking more or less, of the scene presented forty years ago in the little Methodist church at Seneca Falls, the manger in which this organized suffrage movement was born. It was a very small thing then. It was not then big enough to be abused, or loud enough to make itself heard outside, and only a few of those who saw it had any notion that the little thing would live. I have been thinking, too, of the strong conviction, the noble courage, the sublime faith in God and man it required at that time to set this suffrage ball in motion. The history of the world has given to us many sublime undertakings, but none more sublime than this. It was a great thing for the friends of peace to organize in opposition to war; it was a great thing for the friends of temperance to organize against intemperance; it was a great thing for humane people to organize in opposition to slavery; but it was a much greater thing, in view of all the circumstances, for woman to organize herself in opposition to her exclusion from participation in government. The reason is obvious. War, intemperance and slavery are open, undisguised, palpable evils. The best feelings of human nature revolt at them. We could easily make men see the misery, the debasement, the terrible suffering caused by intemperance; we could easily make men see the desolation wrought by war and the hell-black horrors of chattel slavery; but the case was different in the movement for woman suffrage. Men took for granted all that could be said against intemperance, war and slavery. But no such advantage was found in the beginning of the cause of suffrage for women. On the contrary, everything in her condition was supposed to be lovely, just as it should be. She had no rights denied, no wrongs to redress. She herself had no suspicion but that all was going well with her. She floated along on the tide of life as her mother and grandmother had done before her, as in a dream of Paradise. Her wrongs, if she had any, were too occult to be seen, and too light to be felt. It required a daring voice and a determined hand to awake her from this delightful dream and call the nation to account for the rights and opportunities of which it was depriving her. It was well understood at the beginning that woman would not thank us for disturbing her by this call to duty, and it was known that man would denounce and scorn us for such a daring innovation upon the established order of things. But this did not appall or delay the word and work.

"At this distance of time from that convention at Rochester, and in view of the present position of the question, it is hard to realize the moral courage it required to launch this unwelcome movement. Any man can be brave when the danger is over, go to the front when there is no resistance, rejoice when the battle is fought and the victory is won; but it is not so easy to venture upon a field untried with one-half the whole world against you, as these women did.

"Then who were we, for I count myself in, who did this thing? We were few in numbers, moderate in resources, and very little known in the world. The most that we had to commend us was a firm conviction that we were in the right, and a firm faith that the right must ultimately prevail. But the case was well considered. Let no man imagine that the step was taken recklessly and thoughtlessly. Mrs. Stanton had dwelt upon it at least six years before she declared it in the Rochester convention. Walking with her from the house of Joseph and Thankful Southwick, two of the noblest people I ever knew, Mrs. Stanton, with an earnestness that I shall never forget, unfolded her view on this woman question precisely as she had in this Council. This was six and forty years ago, and it was not until six years after, that she ventured to make her formal, pronounced and startling demand for the ballot. She had, as I have said, considered well, and knew something of what would be the cost of the reform she was inaugurating. She knew the ridicule, the rivalry, the criticism and the bitter aspersions which she and her co-laborers would have to meet and to endure. But she saw more clearly than most of us that the vital point to be made prominent, and the one that included all others, was the ballot, and she bravely said the word. It was not only necessary to break the silence of woman and make her voice heard, but she must have a clear, palpable and comprehensive measure set before her, one worthy of her highest ambition and her best exertions, and hence the ballot was brought to the front.

"There are few facts in my humble history to which I look back with more satisfaction than to the fact, recorded in the history of the woman-suffrage movement, that I was sufficiently enlightened at that early day, and when only a few years from slavery, to support your resolution for woman suffrage. I have done very little in this world in which to glory except this one act—and I certainly glory in that. When I ran away from slavery, it was for myself; when I advocated emancipation, it was for my people; but when I stood up for the rights of woman, self was out of the question, and I found a little nobility in the act.

"In estimating the forces with which this suffrage cause has had to contend during these forty years, the fact should be remembered that relations of long standing beget a character in the parties to them in favor of their continuance. Time itself is a conservative power—a very conservative power. One shake of his hoary locks will sometimes paralyze the hand and palsy the tongue of the reformer. The relation of man to woman has the advantage to tell us that what is always was and always will be, world without end. But we have heard this old argument before, and if we live very long we shall hear it again. When any aged error shall be assailed, and any old abuse is to be removed, we shall meet this same old argument. Man has been so long the king and woman the subject—man has been so long accustomed to command and woman to obey—that both parties to the relation have been hardened into their respective places, and thus has been piled up a mountain of iron against woman's enfranchisement.

"The same thing confronted us in our conflicts with slavery. Long years ago Henry Clay said, on the floor of the American Senate, 'I know there is a visionary dogma that man cannot hold property in man,' and, with a brow of defiance, he said, 'That is property which the law makes property. Two hundred years of legislation has sanctioned and sanctified Negro slaves as property.' But neither the power of time nor the might of legislation has been able to keep life in that stupendous barbarism.

"The universality of man's rule over woman is another factor in the resistance to the woman-suffrage movement. We are pointed to the fact that men have not only always ruled over women, but that they do so rule everywhere, and they easily think that a thing that is done everywhere must be right. Though the fallacy of this reasoning is too transparent to need refutation, it still exerts a powerful influence. Even our good Brother Jasper yet believes, with the ancient Church, that the sun 'do move,' notwithstanding all the astronomers of the world are against him. One year ago I stood on the Pincio in Rome and witnessed the unveiling of the statue of Galileo. It was an imposing sight. At no time before had Rome been free enough to permit such a statue to be placed within her walls. It is now there, not with the approval of the Vatican. No priest took part in the ceremonies. It was all the work of laymen. One or two priests passed the statue with averted eyes, but the great truths of the solar system were not angry at the sight, and the same will be true when woman shall be clothed, as she will yet be, with all the rights of American citizenship.

"All good causes are mutually helpful. The benefits accruing from this movement for the equal rights of woman are not confined or limited to woman only. They will be shared by every effort to promote the progress and welfare of mankind every where and in all ages. It was an example and a prophecy of what can be accomplished against strongly opposing forces, against time-hallowed abuses, against deeply entrenched error, against worldwide usage, and against the settled judgment of mankind, by a few earnest women, clad only in the panoply of truth, and determined to live and die in what they considered a righteous cause.

"I do not forget the thoughtful remark of our president in the opening address to this International Council, reminding us of the incompleteness of our work. The remark was wise and timely. Nevertheless, no man can compare the present with the past, the obstacles that then opposed us, and the influences that now favor us, the meeting in the little Methodist chapel forty years ago, and the Council in this vast theater today, without admitting that woman's cause is already a brilliant success. But, however this may be and whatever the future may have in store for us, one thing is certain—this new revolution in human thought will never go backward. When a great truth once gets abroad in the world, no power on earth can imprison it, or prescribe its limits, or suppress it. It is bound to go on till it becomes the thought of the world. Such a truth is woman's right to equal liberty with man. She was born with it. It was hers before she comprehended it. It is inscribed upon all the powers and faculties of her soul, and no custom, law or usage can ever destroy it. Now that it has got fairly fixed in the minds of the few, it is bound to become fixed in the minds of the many, and be supported at last by a great cloud of witnesses, which no man can number and no power can withstand.

"The women who have thus far carried on this agitation have already embodied and illustrated Theodore Parker's three grades of human greatness. The first is greatness in executive and administrative ability; second, greatness in the ability to organize; and, thirdly, in the ability to discover truth. Wherever these three elements of power are combined in any movement, there is a reasonable ground to believe in its final success; and these elements of power have been manifest in the women who have had the movement in hand from the beginning. They are seen in the order which has characterized the proceedings of this Council. They are seen in the depth and are seen in the fervid eloquence and downright earnestness with which women advocate their cause. They are seen in the profound attention with which woman is heard in her own behalf. They are seen in the steady growth and onward march of the movement, and they will be seen in the final triumph of woman's cause, not only in this country, but throughout the world." (Frederick Douglass, *Woman's Journal*, April 14, 1888)

CHAPTER II

My master's family consisted of two sons, Andrew and Richard; one daughter, Lucretia, and her husband, Captain Thomas Auld. They lived in one house, upon the home plantation of Colonel Edward Lloyd. My master was Colonel Lloyd's clerk and superintendent. He was what might be called the overseer[36] of the overseers. I spent two years of childhood on this plantation in my old master's family. It was here that I witnessed the bloody transaction recorded in the first chapter; and as I received my first impressions of slavery on this plantation, I will give some description of it, and of slavery as it there existed. The plantation is about twelve miles north of Easton, in Talbot county, and is situated on the border of Miles River. The principal products raised upon it were tobacco, corn, and wheat. These were raised in great abundance; so that, with the products of this and the other farms belonging to him, he was able to keep in almost constant employment a large sloop, in carrying them to market at Baltimore. This sloop was named Sally Lloyd, in honor of one of the colonel's daughters. My master's son-in-law, Captain Auld, was master of the vessel; she was otherwise manned by the colonel's own slaves. Their names were Peter, Isaac, Rich, and Jake. These were esteemed very highly by the other slaves, and looked upon as the privileged ones of the plantation; for it was no small affair, in the eyes of the slaves, to be allowed to see Baltimore.

Colonel Lloyd kept from three to four hundred slaves on his home plantation, and owned a large number more on the neighboring farms belonging to him. The names of the farms nearest to the home plantation were Wye Town and New Design. "Wye Town" was under the overseership of a man named Noah Willis. New Design was under the overseership of a Mr. Townsend. The overseers of these, and all the rest of the farms, numbering over twenty, received advice and direction from the managers of the home plantation. This was the great business place. It was the seat of government for the whole twenty farms. All disputes among the overseers were settled here. If a slave was convicted of any high misdemeanor, became unmanageable, or evinced a determination to run away, he was brought immediately here, severely whipped, put on board the sloop, carried to Baltimore, and sold to Austin Woolfolk, or some other slave-trader, as a warning to the slaves remaining.

Here, too, the slaves of all the other farms received their monthly allowance of food, and their yearly clothing. The men and women slaves received, as their monthly allowance of food, eight pounds of pork, or its equivalent in fish, and one bushel of corn meal. Their yearly clothing

---

36. The turnover among overseers was high, as was their rate of alcoholism.

consisted of two coarse linen shirts, one pair of linen trousers, like the shirts, one jacket, one pair of trousers for winter, made of coarse negro cloth,[37] one pair of stockings, and one pair of shoes; the whole of which could not have cost more than seven dollars. The allowance of the slave children was given to their mothers, or the old women having the care of them. The children unable to work in the field had neither shoes, stockings, jackets, nor trousers, given to them; their clothing consisted of two coarse linen shirts per year. When these failed them, they went naked until the next allowance-day. Children from seven to ten years old, of both sexes, almost naked, might be seen at all seasons of the year.

There were no beds given the slaves, unless one coarse blanket be considered such, and none but the men and women had these. This, however, is not considered a very great privation. They find less difficulty from the want of beds, than from the want of time to sleep; for when their day's work in the field is done, the most of them having their washing, mending, and cooking to do, and having few or none of the ordinary facilities for doing either of these, very many of their sleeping hours are consumed in preparing for the field the coming day; and when this is done, old and young, male and female, married and single, drop down side by side, on one common bed,—the cold, damp floor,—each covering himself or herself with their miserable blankets; and here they sleep till they are summoned to the field by the driver's horn. At the sound of this, all must rise, and be off to the field. There must be no halting; every one must be at his or her post; and woe betides them who hear not this morning summons to the field; for if they are not awakened by the sense of hearing, they are by the sense of feeling: no age nor sex finds any favor. Mr. Severe, the overseer, used to stand by the door of the quarter, armed with a large hickory stick and heavy cowskin, ready to whip any one who was so unfortunate as not to hear, or, from any other cause, was prevented from being ready to start for the field at the sound of the horn.

Mr. Severe was rightly named: he was a cruel man. I have seen him whip a woman, causing the blood to run half an hour at the time; and this, too, in the midst of her crying children, pleading for their mother's release. He seemed to take pleasure in manifesting his fiendish barbarity. Added to his cruelty, he was a profane swearer. It was enough to chill the blood and stiffen the hair of an ordinary man to hear him talk. Scarce a sentence escaped him but that was commenced or concluded by some horrid oath. The field was the place to witness his cruelty and profanity. His presence made it both the field of blood and of blasphemy. From the rising till the going down of the sun, he was cursing, raving, cutting, and slashing among

---

37. Often made of rough, unbleached cotton.

the slaves of the field, in the most frightful manner. His career was short. He died very soon after I went to Colonel Lloyd's; and he died as he lived, uttering, with his dying groans, bitter curses and horrid oaths. His death was regarded by the slaves as the result of a merciful providence.

Mr. Severe's place was filled by a Mr. Hopkins. He was a very different man. He was less cruel, less profane, and made less noise, than Mr. Severe. His course was characterized by no extraordinary demonstrations of cruelty. He whipped, but seemed to take no pleasure in it. He was called by the slaves a good overseer.

The home plantation of Colonel Lloyd wore the appearance of a country village. All the mechanical operations for all the farms were performed here. The shoemaking and mending, the blacksmithing, cartwrighting, coopering, weaving, and grain-grinding, were all performed by the slaves on the home plantation. The whole place wore a business-like aspect very unlike the neighboring farms. The number of houses, too, conspired to give it advantage over the neighboring farms. It was called by the slaves the Great House Farm. Few privileges were esteemed higher, by the slaves of the out-farms, than that of being selected to do errands at the Great House Farm. It was associated in their minds with greatness. A representative could not be prouder of his election to a seat in the American Congress, than a slave on one of the out-farms would be of his election to do errands at the *Great House Farm.* They regarded it as evidence of great confidence reposed in them by their overseers; and it was on this account, as well as a constant desire to be out of the field from under the driver's lash, that they esteemed it a high privilege, one worth careful living for. He was called the smartest and most trusty fellow, who had this honor conferred upon him the most frequently. The competitors for this office sought as diligently to please their overseers, as the office-seekers in the political parties seek to please and deceive the people. The same traits of character might be seen in Colonel Lloyd's slaves, as are seen in the slaves of the political parties.[38]

The slaves selected to go to the Great House Farm, for the monthly allowance for themselves and their fellow-slaves, were peculiarly enthusiastic. While on their way, they would make the dense old woods, for miles around, reverberate with their wild songs, revealing at once the highest joy and the deepest sadness. They would compose and sing as they went along, consulting neither time nor tune. The thought that came up, came out—if not in the word, in the sound;—and as frequently in

---

38. Slaves invited to the "Big House" saw the world differently from the way slaves working in the fields did. Some house slaves could be relied on to inform the masters about what was going on in the quarters, for example.

the one as in the other. They would sometimes sing the most pathetic sentiment in the most rapturous tone, and the most rapturous sentiment in the most pathetic tone. Into all of their songs they would manage to weave something of the Great House Farm. Especially would they do this, when leaving home. They would then sing most exultingly the following words:—

> "I am going away to the Great House Farm!
> O, yea! O, yea! O!"

This they would sing, as a chorus, to words which to many would seem unmeaning jargon, but which, nevertheless, were full of meaning to themselves. I have sometimes thought that the mere hearing of those songs would do more to impress some minds with the horrible character of slavery, than the reading of whole volumes of philosophy on the subject could do.

I did not, when a slave, understand the deep meaning of those rude and apparently incoherent songs. I was myself within the circle; so that I neither saw nor heard as those without might see and hear. They told a tale of woe which was then altogether beyond my feeble comprehension; they were tones loud, long, and deep; they breathed the prayer and complaint of souls boiling over with the bitterest anguish. Every tone was a testimony against slavery, and a prayer to God for deliverance from chains. The hearing of those wild notes always depressed my spirit, and filled me with ineffable sadness. I have frequently found myself in tears while hearing them. The mere recurrence to those songs, even now, afflicts me; and while I am writing these lines, an expression of feeling has already found its way down my cheek. To those songs I trace my first glimmering conception of the dehumanizing character of slavery. I can never get rid of that conception. Those songs still follow me, to deepen my hatred of slavery, and quicken my sympathies for my brethren in bonds. If any one wishes to be impressed with the soul-killing effects of slavery, let him go to Colonel Lloyd's plantation, and, on allowance-day, place himself in the deep pine woods, and there let him, in silence, analyze the sounds that shall pass through the chambers of his soul,—and if he is not thus impressed, it will only be because "there is no flesh in his obdurate heart."[39]

I have often been utterly astonished, since I came to the north, to find persons who could speak of the singing, among slaves, as evidence of their contentment and happiness. It is impossible to conceive of a greater

---

39. William Cowper, *The Task*, 1785.

mistake. Slaves sing most when they are most unhappy. The songs of the slave represent the sorrows of his heart; and he is relieved by them, only as an aching heart is relieved by its tears. At least, such is my experience. I have often sung to drown my sorrow, but seldom to express my happiness. Crying for joy, and singing for joy, were alike uncommon to me while in the jaws of slavery. The singing of a man cast away upon a desolate island might be as appropriately considered as evidence of contentment and happiness, as the singing of a slave; the songs of the one and of the other are prompted by the same emotion.

CHAPTER III

COLONEL Lloyd kept a large and finely cultivated garden,[40] which afforded almost constant employment for four men, besides the chief gardener, (Mr. M'Durmond.) This garden was probably the greatest attraction of the place. During the summer months, people came from far and near— from Baltimore, Easton, and Annapolis—to see it. It abounded in fruits of almost every description, from the hardy apple of the north to the delicate orange of the south. This garden was not the least source of trouble on the plantation. Its excellent fruit was quite a temptation to the hungry swarms of boys, as well as the older slaves, belonging to the colonel, few of whom had the virtue or the vice to resist it. Scarcely a day passed, during the summer, but that some slave had to take the lash for stealing fruit. The colonel had to resort to all kinds of stratagems to keep his slaves out of the garden. The last and most successful one was that of tarring his fence all around; after which, if a slave was caught with any tar upon his person, it was deemed sufficient proof that he had either been into the garden, or had tried to get in. In either case, he was severely whipped by the chief gardener. This plan worked well; the slaves became as fearful of tar as of the lash. They seemed to realize the impossibility of touching tar without being defiled.

---

40. Colonel Lloyd's garden and the tarred fence around it is one of the most suggestive images in the *Narrative*: it reminds us of the Garden of Eden in Genesis with its forbidden fruit and punishment for those who eat it, gardens as places of contemplation and retreat, tarring and feathering, tarring everyone with the same brush, and the tarbaby story (people who hit it got stuck to it); this image may also contain a resonant prospective irony in that Colonel Lloyd's garden suggests peace and harmony in a state that in sixteen years after the publication of Douglass's *Narrative* in 1845, will be involved in the bloodiest war in United States history. Colonel Lloyd's slaves had to toil in his garden, but they were not allowed to enjoy the fruit of their labors.

The colonel also kept a splendid riding equipage. His stable and carriage-house presented the appearance of some of our large city livery establishments. His horses were of the finest form and noblest blood. His carriage-house contained three splendid coaches, three or four gigs, besides dearborns and barouches of the most fashionable style.

This establishment was under the care of two slaves—old Barney and young Barney—father and son. To attend to this establishment was their sole work. But it was by no means an easy employment; for in nothing was Colonel Lloyd more particular than in the management of his horses.[41] The slightest inattention to these was unpardonable, and was visited upon those, under whose care they were placed, with the severest punishment; no excuse could shield them, if the colonel only suspected any want of attention to his horses—a supposition which he frequently indulged, and one which, of course, made the office of old and young Barney a very trying one. They never knew when they were safe from punishment. They were frequently whipped when least deserving, and escaped whipping when most deserving it. Every thing depended upon the looks of the horses, and the state of Colonel Lloyd's own mind when his horses were brought to him for use. If a horse did not move fast enough, or hold his head high enough, it was owing to some fault of his keepers. It was painful to stand near the stable-door, and hear the various complaints against the keepers when a horse was taken out for use. "This horse has not had proper attention. He has not been sufficiently rubbed and curried, or he has not been properly fed; his food was too wet or too dry; he got it too soon or too late; he was too hot or too cold; he had too much hay, and not enough of grain; or he had too much grain, and not enough of hay; instead of old Barney's attending to the horse, he had very improperly left it to his son." To all these complaints, no matter how unjust, the slave must answer never a word. Colonel Lloyd could not brook any contradiction from a slave. When he spoke, a slave must stand, listen, and tremble; and such was literally the case. I have seen Colonel Lloyd make old Barney, a man between fifty and sixty years of age, uncover his bald head, kneel down upon the cold, damp ground, and receive upon his naked and toil-worn shoulders more than thirty lashes at the time. Colonel Lloyd had three sons—Edward, Murray, and Daniel,—and three sons-in-law, Mr. Winder, Mr. Nicholson, and Mr. Lowndes. All of these lived at the Great House Farm, and enjoyed the luxury of whipping the servants when they pleased, from old Barney down to William Wilkes, the coach-driver. I have seen Winder make one of the house-servants stand

---

41. Colonel Lloyd's horses mean far more to him than the humans he owns do because he does not empathize with them; his slaves are more on the order of pigs in his hierarchy of beings.

off from him a suitable distance to be touched with the end of his whip, and at every stroke raise great ridges upon his back.

To describe the wealth of Colonel Lloyd would be almost equal to describing the riches of Job.[42] He kept from ten to fifteen house-servants. He was said to own a thousand slaves, and I think this estimate quite within the truth. Colonel Lloyd owned so many that he did not know them when he saw them; nor did all the slaves of the out-farms know him. It is reported of him, that, while riding along the road one day, he met a colored man, and addressed him in the usual manner of speaking to colored people on the public highways of the south: "Well, boy, whom do you belong to?" "To Colonel Lloyd," replied the slave. "Well, does the colonel treat you well?" "No, sir," was the ready reply. "What, does he work you too hard?" "Yes, sir." "Well, don't he give you enough to eat?" "Yes, sir, he gives me enough, such as it is."[43]

The colonel, after ascertaining where the slave belonged, rode on; the man also went on about his business, not dreaming that he had been conversing with his master. He thought, said, and heard nothing more of the matter, until two or three weeks afterwards. The poor man was then informed by his overseer that, for having found fault with his master, he was now to be sold to a Georgia trader. He was immediately chained and handcuffed; and thus, without a moment's warning, he was snatched away, and forever sundered, from his family and friends, by a hand more unrelenting than death. This is the penalty of telling the truth, of telling the simple truth, in answer to a series of plain questions.

It is partly in consequence of such facts, that slaves, when inquired of as to their condition and the character of their masters, almost universally say they are contented, and that their masters are kind. The slaveholders have been known to send in spies among their slaves, to ascertain their views and feelings in regard to their condition. The frequency of this has had the effect to establish among the slaves the maxim, that a still tongue makes a wise head. They suppress the truth rather than take the consequences of telling it, and in so doing prove themselves a part of the human family. If they have any thing to say of their masters, it is generally in their masters' favor, especially when speaking to an untried man. I have been frequently asked, when a slave, if I had a kind master, and do not

---

42. In the King James Version of the Bible (Job 1:3), Job is said to have "several thousand sheep, and three thousand camels, and five hundred yoke of oxen, and five hundred she asses, and a very great household; so that this man was the greatest of all the men of the earth."

43. Contemporary readers may wonder if a slave would have answered an unknown white man's question so honestly, when the result could have been severe punishment.

remember ever to have given a negative answer; nor did I, in pursuing this course, consider myself as uttering what was absolutely false; for I always measured the kindness of my master by the standard of kindness set up among slaveholders around us. Moreover, slaves are like other people, and imbibe prejudices quite common to others. They think their own better than that of others. Many, under the influence of this prejudice, think their own masters are better than the masters of other slaves; and this, too, in some cases, when the very reverse is true. Indeed, it is not uncommon for slaves even to fall out and quarrel among themselves about the relative goodness of their masters, each contending for the superior goodness of his own over that of the others. At the very same time, they mutually execrate their masters when viewed separately. It was so on our plantation. When Colonel Lloyd's slaves met the slaves of Jacob Jepson,[44] they seldom parted without a quarrel about their masters; Colonel Lloyd's slaves contending that he was the richest, and Mr. Jepson's slaves that he was the smartest, and most of a man. Colonel Lloyd's slaves would boast his ability to buy and sell Jacob Jepson. Mr. Jepson's slaves would boast his ability to whip Colonel Lloyd. These quarrels would almost always end in a fight between the parties, and those that whipped were supposed to have gained the point at issue. They seemed to think that the greatness of their masters was transferable to themselves. It was considered as being bad enough to be a slave; but to be a poor man's slave was deemed a disgrace indeed!

CHAPTER IV

Mr. Hopkins remained but a short time in the office of overseer. Why his career was so short, I do not know, but suppose he lacked the necessary severity to suit Colonel Lloyd. Mr. Hopkins was succeeded by Mr. Austin Gore,[45] a man possessing, in an eminent degree, all those traits of character indispensable to what is called a first-rate overseer. Mr. Gore had served Colonel Lloyd, in the capacity of overseer, upon one

---

44. Actually Jacob Gibson, according to Preston, *Young Frederick Douglass*, 60, 221, note 28.

45. Austin Gore was even more depraved than Mr. Covey, the overseer Douglass fights in Chapter VIII. The former seems to have found murdering the slave named Demby nowhere near his conscience; in fact he revels in it. And, as Douglass points out, there were no consequences to Gore's utter brutality whatsoever. Gore emerges from the *Narrative* as a symbol of the unrestrained violence that slavery was based on.

of the out-farms, and had shown himself worthy of the high station of overseer upon the home or Great House Farm.

Mr. Gore was proud, ambitious, and persevering. He was artful, cruel, and obdurate. He was just the man for such a place, and it was just the place for such a man. It afforded scope for the full exercise of all his powers, and he seemed to be perfectly at home in it. He was one of those who could torture the slightest look, word, or gesture, on the part of the slave, into impudence, and would treat it accordingly. There must be no answering back to him; no explanation was allowed a slave, showing himself to have been wrongfully accused. Mr. Gore acted fully up to the maxim laid down by slaveholders,—"It is better that a dozen slaves should suffer under the lash, than that the overseer should be convicted, in the presence of the slaves, of having been at fault." No matter how innocent a slave might be—it availed him nothing, when accused by Mr. Gore of any misdemeanor. To be accused was to be convicted, and to be convicted was to be punished; the one always following the other with immutable certainty. To escape punishment was to escape accusation; and few slaves had the fortune to do either, under the overseership of Mr. Gore. He was just proud enough to demand the most debasing homage of the slave, and quite servile enough to crouch, himself, at the feet of the master. He was ambitious enough to be contented with nothing short of the highest rank of overseers, and persevering enough to reach the height of his ambition. He was cruel enough to inflict the severest punishment, artful enough to descend to the lowest trickery, and obdurate enough to be insensible to the voice of a reproving conscience. He was, of all the overseers, the most dreaded by the slaves. His presence was painful; his eye flashed confusion; and seldom was his sharp, shrill voice heard, without producing horror and trembling in their ranks.

Mr. Gore was a grave man, and, though a young man, he indulged in no jokes, said no funny words, seldom smiled. His words were in perfect keeping with his looks, and his looks were in perfect keeping with his words. Overseers will sometimes indulge in a witty word, even with the slaves; not so with Mr. Gore. He spoke but to command, and commanded but to be obeyed; he dealt sparingly with his words, and bountifully with his whip, never using the former where the latter would answer as well. When he whipped, he seemed to do so from a sense of duty, and feared no consequences. He did nothing reluctantly, no matter how disagreeable; always at his post, never inconsistent. He never promised but to fulfil. He was, in a word, a man of the most inflexible firmness and stone-like coolness.

His savage barbarity was equalled only by the consummate coolness with which he committed the grossest and most savage deeds upon the slaves under his charge. Mr. Gore once undertook to whip one of Colonel

Lloyd's slaves, by the name of Demby.[46] He had given Demby but few stripes, when, to get rid of the scourging, he ran and plunged himself into a creek, and stood there at the depth of his shoulders, refusing to come out. Mr. Gore told him that he would give him three calls, and that, if he did not come out at the third call, he would shoot him. The first call was given. Demby made no response, but stood his ground. The second and third calls were given with the same result. Mr. Gore then, without consultation or deliberation with any one, not even giving Demby an additional call, raised his musket to his face, taking deadly aim at his standing victim, and in an instant poor Demby was no more. His mangled body sank out of sight, and blood and brains marked the water where he had stood.

A thrill of horror flashed through every soul upon the plantation, excepting Mr. Gore. He alone seemed cool and collected. He was asked by Colonel Lloyd and my old master, why he resorted to this extraordinary expedient. His reply was, (as well as I can remember,) that Demby had become unmanageable. He was setting a dangerous example to the other slaves,—one which, if suffered to pass without some such demonstration on his part, would finally lead to the total subversion of all rule and order upon the plantation. He argued that if one slave refused to be corrected, and escaped with his life, the other slaves would soon copy the example; the result of which would be, the freedom of the slaves, and the enslavement of the whites. Mr. Gore's defence was satisfactory. He was continued in his station as overseer upon the home plantation. His fame as an overseer went abroad. His horrid crime was not even submitted to judicial investigation. It was committed in the presence of slaves, and they of course could neither institute a suit, nor testify against him; and thus the guilty perpetrator of one of the bloodiest and most foul murders goes unwhipped of justice, and uncensured by the community in which he lives. Mr. Gore lived in St. Michael's, Talbot county, Maryland, when I left there; and if he is still alive, he very probably lives there now; and if so, he is now, as he was then, as highly esteemed and as much respected as though his guilty soul had not been stained with his brother's blood.

I speak advisedly when I say this,—that killing a slave, or any colored person, in Talbot county, Maryland, is not treated as a crime, either by the courts or the community. Mr. Thomas Lanman, of St. Michael's, killed two slaves, one of whom he killed with a hatchet, by knocking his brains out. He used to boast of the commission of the awful and bloody deed. I have heard him do so laughingly, saying, among other things, that he was

---

46. Douglass would have been a little boy when Demby was shot by Gore, which contributed to the atmosphere of racial terror and intimidation Douglass grew up in.

the only benefactor of his country in the company, and that when others would do as much as he had done, we should be relieved of "the d——d niggers."

The wife of Mr. Giles Hicks, living but a short distance from where I used to live, murdered my wife's[47] cousin, a young girl between fifteen and sixteen years of age, mangling her person in the most horrible manner, breaking her nose and breastbone with a stick, so that the poor girl expired in a few hours afterward. She was immediately buried, but had not been in her untimely grave but a few hours before she was taken up and examined by the coroner, who decided that she had come to her death by severe beating. The offence for which this girl was thus murdered was this:—She had been set that night to mind Mrs. Hicks's baby, and during the night she fell asleep, and the baby cried. She, having lost her rest for several nights previous, did not hear the crying. They were both in the room with Mrs. Hicks. Mrs. Hicks, finding the girl slow to move, jumped from her bed, seized an oak stick of wood by the fireplace, and with it broke the girl's nose and breastbone, and thus ended her life. I will not say that this most horrid murder produced no sensation in the community. It did produce sensation, but not enough to bring the murderess to punishment. There was a warrant issued for her arrest, but it was never served. Thus she escaped not only punishment, but even the pain of being arraigned before a court for her horrid crime.

Whilst I am detailing bloody deeds which took place during my stay on Colonel Lloyd's plantation, I will briefly narrate another, which occurred about the same time as the murder of Demby by Mr. Gore.

Colonel Lloyd's slaves were in the habit of spending a part of their nights and Sundays in fishing for oysters, and in this way made up the deficiency of their scanty allowance. An old man belonging to Colonel Lloyd, while thus engaged, happened to get beyond the limits of Colonel Lloyd's, and on the premises of Mr. Beal Bondly. At this trespass, Mr. Bondly took offence, and with his musket came down to the shore, and blew its deadly contents into the poor old man.

Mr. Bondly came over to see Colonel Lloyd the next day, whether to pay him for his property, or to justify himself in what he had done, I know not. At any rate, this whole fiendish transaction was soon hushed up. There

---

47. This is a reference to Douglass's first wife, a free black woman named Anna Murray who helped Douglass escape from slavery. Barely literate, she could not leave a written record of her relationship with Douglass, which would fill a huge gap in the *Narrative*, where she is seldom mentioned. She was one of the key women in Douglass's life, though, along with his mother Harriet Bailey, his second wife Helen Pitts, and his German friend Ottilie Assing.

was very little said about it at all, and nothing done. It was a common saying, even among little white boys, that it was worth a half-cent to kill a
"nigger," and a half-cent to bury one.

CHAPTER V

As to my own treatment while I lived on Colonel Lloyd's plantation,
it was very similar to that of the other slave children. I was not old enough
to work in the field, and there being little else than field work to do, I had
a great deal of leisure time. The most I had to do was to drive up the cows
at evening, keep the fowls out of the garden, keep the front yard clean, and
run of errands for my old master's daughter, Mrs. Lucretia Auld. The most
of my leisure time I spent in helping Master Daniel Lloyd in finding his
birds, after he had shot them. My connection with Master Daniel was of
some advantage to me. He became quite attached to me, and was a sort of
protector of me. He would not allow the older boys to impose upon me,
and would divide his cakes with me.

I was seldom whipped by my old master, and suffered little from any
thing else than hunger and cold. I suffered much from hunger, but much
more from cold. In hottest summer and coldest winter, I was kept almost
naked—no shoes, no stockings, no jacket, no trousers, nothing on but a
coarse tow linen shirt, reaching only to my knees. I had no bed. I must
have perished with cold, but that, the coldest nights, I used to steal a bag
which was used for carrying corn to the mill. I would crawl into this bag,
and there sleep on the cold, damp, clay floor, with my head in and feet out.
My feet have been so cracked with the frost, that the pen with which I am
writing might be laid in the gashes.[48]

---

48. One of the most resonant images in the *Narrative*. It combines literacy with the
unspeakable suffering Douglass and his fellow slaves had to endure. The poignancy of the
image of the tool that enabled Douglass to represent slavery so eloquently being placed in
the pain caused by slavery, is almost unbearable. The image is what Douglass did throughout
his writing career: use literacy to stop the pain of slavery. This image is a kind of literary
mascon: a mascon (from 'mass construction') is an area of excess gravitational energy on
the moon, caused by asteroids that have penetrated the moon's surface and remained un-
derneath it, thereby creating a surface area of unexpectedly high gravitation. Similarly, Douglass's hyperresonant image of gashes so deep in his feet that they could accommodate his
pen is a powerful sign of his entire body of work, not just his 1845 *Narrative*. With its excess
of moral and literary energy, it vividly conveys the concept that America has citizens so
badly wounded that many volumes and centuries will be required before the pain can be
understood and ended. And yet Douglass was demanding only that America treat its black
citizens no worse than it treat its enemies.

We were not regularly allowanced. Our food was coarse corn meal boiled. This was called mush. It was put into a large wooden tray or trough, and set down upon the ground. The children were then called, like so many pigs, and like so many pigs they would come and devour the mush; some with oyster-shells, others with pieces of shingle, some with naked hands, and none with spoons. He that ate fastest got most; he that was strongest secured the best place; and few left the trough satisfied.

I was probably between seven and eight years old when I left Colonel Lloyd's plantation. I left it with joy. I shall never forget the ecstasy with which I received the intelligence that my old master (Anthony) had determined to let me go to Baltimore, to live with Mr. Hugh Auld, brother to my old master's son-in-law, Captain Thomas Auld. I received this information about three days before my departure. They were three of the happiest days I ever enjoyed. I spent the most part of all these three days in the creek, washing off the plantation scurf,[49] and preparing myself for my departure.

The pride of appearance[50] which this would indicate was not my own. I spent the time in washing, not so much because I wished to, but because Mrs. Lucretia had told me I must get all the dead skin off my feet and knees before I could go to Baltimore; for the people in Baltimore were very cleanly, and would laugh at me if I looked dirty. Besides, she was going to give me a pair of trousers, which I should not put on unless I got all the dirt off me. The thought of owning a pair of trousers was great indeed! It was almost a sufficient motive, not only to make me take off what would be called by pig-drovers the mange,[51] but the skin itself. I went at it in good earnest, working for the first time with the hope of reward.

The ties that ordinarily bind children to their homes were all suspended in my case. I found no severe trial in my departure. My home was charmless; it was not home to me; on parting from it, I could not feel that I was leaving any thing which I could have enjoyed by staying. My mother was

---

49. Flaky deposit or dead skin, dandruff.

50. Douglass was always very concerned with his appearance. In a century in which photography became increasingly important in the construction of identity, he sat for his picture numerous times, as did many other luminaries, such as Lincoln and Whitman. With his robust ego and tremendous sense of presence and dignity, Douglass was born to be photographed. His writing style also reflects these qualities; in other words, Douglass looked like and wrote like a man. As Maurice Wallace points out in his essay in *Frederick Douglass & Herman Melville, Essays in Relation*, Douglass intentionally chose to wear clothes that suggest a military uniform partly because two of his sons were soldiers in the Union Army and he did not want them to eclipse him (photographs of them in uniform were made) and also because he was trying to compensate visually for the fact that he never received a promised commission as a Union officer.

51. Skin disease caused by mites.

dead, my grandmother lived far off, so that I seldom saw her. I had two sisters and one brother,[52] that lived in the same house with me; but the early separation of us from our mother had well nigh blotted the fact of our relationship from our memories. I looked for home elsewhere, and was confident of finding none which I should relish less than the one which I was leaving. If, however, I found in my new home hardship, hunger, whipping, and nakedness, I had the consolation that I should not have escaped any one of them by staying. Having already had more than a taste of them in the house of my old master, and having endured them there, I very naturally inferred my ability to endure them elsewhere, and especially at Baltimore; for I had something of the feeling about Baltimore that is expressed in the proverb, that "being hanged in England is preferable to dying a natural death in Ireland." I had the strongest desire to see Baltimore. Cousin Tom, though not fluent in speech, had inspired me with that desire by his eloquent description of the place. I could never point out any thing at the Great House, no matter how beautiful or powerful, but that he had seen something at Baltimore far exceeding, both in beauty and strength, the object which I pointed out to him. Even the Great House itself, with all its pictures, was far inferior to many buildings in Baltimore. So strong was my desire, that I thought a gratification of it would fully compensate for whatever loss of comforts I should sustain by the exchange. I left without a regret, and with the highest hopes of future happiness.

We sailed out of Miles River for Baltimore on a Saturday morning. I remember only the day of the week, for at that time I had no knowledge of the days of the month, nor the months of the year. On setting sail, I walked aft, and gave to Colonel Lloyd's plantation what I hoped would be the last look. I then placed myself in the bows of the sloop, and there spent the remainder of the day in looking ahead, interesting myself in what was in the distance rather than in things near by or behind.

In the afternoon of that day, we reached Annapolis, the capital of the State. We stopped but a few moments, so that I had no time to go on shore. It was the first large town that I had ever seen, and though it would look small compared with some of our New England factory villages, I thought it a wonderful place for its size—more imposing even than the Great House Farm!

We arrived at Baltimore early on Sunday morning, landing at Smith's Wharf, not far from Bowley's Wharf. We had on board the sloop a large flock of sheep; and after aiding in driving them to the slaughterhouse of

---

52. One of the sisters has been identified as Eliza Bailey; the brother was Perry Bailey (*Narrative of the Life of Frederick Douglass*, eds. John W. Blassingame, John R McKivigan, and Peter H. Hinks, p. 104).

Mr. Curtis on Louden Slater's Hill, I was conducted by Rich, one of the hands belonging on board of the sloop, to my new home in Alliciana Street, near Mr. Gardner's ship-yard, on Fells Point.

Mr. and Mrs. Auld were both at home, and met me at the door with their little son Thomas, to take care of whom I had been given. And here I saw what I had never seen before; it was a white face beaming with the most kindly emotions; it was the face of my new mistress, Sophia Auld.[53] I wish I could describe the rapture that flashed through my soul as I beheld it. It was a new and strange sight to me, brightening up my pathway with the light of happiness. Little Thomas was told, there was his Freddy,—and I was told to take care of little Thomas; and thus I entered upon the duties of my new home with the most cheering prospect ahead.

I look upon my departure from Colonel Lloyd's plantation as one of the most interesting events of my life. It is possible, and even quite probable, that but for the mere circumstance of being removed from that plantation to Baltimore, I should have to-day, instead of being here seated by my own table, in the enjoyment of freedom and the happiness of home, writing this Narrative, been confined in the galling chains of slavery. Going to live at Baltimore laid the foundation, and opened the gateway, to all my subsequent prosperity. I have ever regarded it as the first plain manifestation of that kind providence which has ever since attended me, and marked my life with so many favors. I regarded the selection of myself as being somewhat remarkable. There were a number of slave children that might have been sent from the plantation to Baltimore. There were those younger, those older, and those of the same age. I was chosen from among them all, and was the first, last, and only choice.[54]

I may be deemed superstitious, and even egotistical, in regarding this event as a special interposition of divine Providence in my favor. But I should be false to the earliest sentiments of my soul, if I suppressed the opinion. I prefer to be true to myself, even at the hazard of incurring the ridicule of others, rather than to be false, and incur my own abhorrence.

---

53. Douglass's sentimentalization and idealization of Sophia Auld recalls the nineteenth-century American and English idea of the Angel in the House, that is, women were meant to be perfect mothers and wives. Given his affection for her, his disillusionment would have been profound when her power over him resulted in her corruption, although they were still fond of each other years later (see Preston, *Young Frederick Douglass*). She also may have filled a void in Douglass's life resulting from his barely knowing his biological mother.

54. Clearly, Douglass regards himself as a Child of Destiny, someone chosen by Providence for a special purpose, like Moses in the Old Testament, that is, someone destined to lead black Americans out of slavery. Douglass retained this sense of purpose throughout his life.

From my earliest recollection, I date the entertainment of a deep conviction that slavery would not always be able to hold me within its foul embrace; and in the darkest hours of my career in slavery, this living word of faith and spirit of hope departed not from me, but remained like ministering angels to cheer me through the gloom. This good spirit was from God, and to him I offer thanksgiving and praise.

CHAPTER VI

MY new mistress proved to be all she appeared when I first met her at the door,—a woman of the kindest heart and finest feelings. She had never had a slave under her control previously to myself, and prior to her marriage she had been dependent upon her own industry for a living. She was by trade a weaver; and by constant application to her business, she had been in a good degree preserved from the blighting and dehumanizing effects of slavery. I was utterly astonished at her goodness. I scarcely knew how to behave towards her. She was entirely unlike any other white woman I had ever seen. I could not approach her as I was accustomed to approach other white ladies. My early instruction was all out of place. The crouching servility, usually so acceptable a quality in a slave, did not answer when manifested toward her. Her favor was not gained by it; she seemed to be disturbed by it. She did not deem it impudent or unmannerly for a slave to look her in the face. The meanest slave was put fully at ease in her presence, and none left without feeling better for having seen her. Her face was made of heavenly smiles, and her voice of tranquil music.

But, alas! this kind heart had but a short time to remain such. The fatal poison of irresponsible power was already in her hands, and soon commenced its infernal work. That cheerful eye, under the influence of slavery, soon became red with rage; that voice, made all of sweet accord, changed to one of harsh and horrid discord; and that angelic face gave place to that of a demon.[55]

Very soon after I went to live with Mr. and Mrs. Auld, she very kindly commenced to teach me the A, B, C. After I had learned this, she assisted me in learning to spell words of three or four letters. Just at this point of my progress, Mr. Auld found out what was going on, and at once forbade Mrs. Auld to instruct me further, telling her, among other things, that

---

55. But "[b]oth Douglass and Sophia Auld retained enormous affection for one another long after Douglass had established himself in the North. . . . Years after her death, her son told Douglass that "mother would always speak in the kindest terms of you [Douglass], whenever your name was mentioned." (Blassingame, p. 106)

it was unlawful,[56] as well as unsafe, to teach a slave to read. To use his own words, further, he said, "If you give a nigger an inch, he will take an ell.[57] A nigger should know nothing but to obey his master—to do as he is told to do. Learning would spoil the best nigger in the world. Now," said he, "if you teach that nigger (speaking of myself) how to read, there would be no keeping him. It would forever unfit him to be a slave. He would at once become unmanageable, and of no value to his master. As to himself, it could do him no good, but a great deal of harm. It would make him discontented and unhappy." These words sank deep into my heart, stirred up sentiments within that lay slumbering, and called into existence an entirely new train of thought. It was a new and special revelation, explaining dark and mysterious things, with which my youthful understanding had struggled, but struggled in vain. I now understood what had been to me a most perplexing difficulty—to wit, the white man's power to enslave the black man. It was a grand achievement, and I prized it highly. From that moment, I understood the pathway from slavery to freedom. It was just what I wanted, and I got it at a time when I the least expected it. Whilst I was saddened by the thought of losing the aid of my kind mistress, I was gladdened by the invaluable instruction which, by the merest accident, I had gained from my master. Though conscious of the difficulty of learning without a teacher, I set out with high hope, and a fixed purpose, at whatever cost of trouble, to learn how to read. The very decided manner with which he spoke, and strove to impress his wife with the evil consequences of giving me instruction, served to convince me that he was deeply sensible of the truths he was uttering. It gave me the best assurance that I might rely with the utmost confidence on the results which, he said, would flow from teaching me to read. What he most dreaded, that I most desired. What he most loved, that I most hated. That which to him was a great evil, to be carefully shunned, was to me a great good, to be diligently sought; and the argument which he so warmly urged, against my learning to read, only served to inspire me with a desire and determination to learn. In learning to read, I owe almost as much to the bitter opposition of my master, as to the kindly aid of my mistress. I acknowledge the benefit of both.

---

56. Actually, this was not the case in Maryland (Maryland did not join the Confederacy, although slavery was legal in that state). Douglass realized that literacy and freedom were intimately connected, and thus the former was the key to the latter. One of the most ridiculous contradictions in slavery was the nonsensical notion of passing laws against literacy for subhumans: if they are incapable of literacy, why pass laws against it?

57. According to the online Oxford dictionary, an ell is "a former measure of length (equivalent to six hand breadths) used mainly for textiles, locally variable but typically about 45 inches."

I had resided but a short time in Baltimore before I observed a marked difference, in the treatment of slaves, from that which I had witnessed in the country. A city slave is almost a freeman, compared with a slave on the plantation. He is much better fed and clothed, and enjoys privileges altogether unknown to the slave on the plantation. There is a vestige of decency, a sense of shame, that does much to curb and check those outbreaks of atrocious cruelty so commonly enacted upon the plantation. He is a desperate slaveholder, who will shock the humanity of his non-slaveholding neighbors with the cries of his lacerated slave. Few are willing to incur the odium attaching to the reputation of being a cruel master; and above all things, they would not be known as not giving a slave enough to eat. Every city slaveholder is anxious to have it known of him, that he feeds his slaves well; and it is due to them to say, that most of them do give their slaves enough to eat. There are, however, some painful exceptions to this rule. Directly opposite to us, on Philpot Street, lived Mr. Thomas Hamilton. He owned two slaves. Their names were Henrietta and Mary. Henrietta was about twenty-two years of age, Mary was about fourteen; and of all the mangled and emaciated creatures I ever looked upon, these two were the most so. His heart must be harder than stone, that could look upon these unmoved. The head, neck, and shoulders of Mary were literally cut to pieces. I have frequently felt her head, and found it nearly covered with festering sores, caused by the lash of her cruel mistress. I do not know that her master ever whipped her, but I have been an eye-witness to the cruelty of Mrs. Hamilton. I used to be in Mr. Hamilton's house nearly every day. Mrs. Hamilton used to sit in a large chair in the middle of the room, with a heavy cowskin always by her side, and scarce an hour passed during the day but was marked by the blood of one of these slaves. The girls seldom passed her without her saying, "Move faster, you black gip!"[58] at the same time giving them a blow with the cowskin over the head or shoulders, often drawing the blood. She would then say, "Take that, you black gip!" continuing, "If you don't move faster, I'll move you!" Added to the cruel lashings to which these slaves were subjected, they were kept nearly half-starved. They seldom knew what it was to eat a full meal. I have seen Mary contending with the pigs for the offal thrown into the street. So much was Mary kicked and cut to pieces, that she was oftener called "pecked" than by her name.

CHAPTER VII

I lived in Master Hugh's family about seven years. During this time, I succeeded in learning to read and write. In accomplishing this, I was

---

58. Gypsy.

compelled to resort to various stratagems. I had no regular teacher. My mistress, who had kindly commenced to instruct me, had, in compliance with the advice and direction of her husband, not only ceased to instruct, but had set her face against my being instructed by any one else. It is due, however, to my mistress to say of her, that she did not adopt this course of treatment immediately. She at first lacked the depravity indispensable to shutting me up in mental darkness. It was at least necessary for her to have some training in the exercise of irresponsible power, to make her equal to the task of treating me as though I were a brute.

My mistress was, as I have said, a kind and tender-hearted woman; and in the simplicity of her soul she commenced, when I first went to live with her, to treat me as she supposed one human being ought to treat another. In entering upon the duties of a slaveholder, she did not seem to perceive that I sustained to her the relation of a mere chattel, and that for her to treat me as a human being was not only wrong, but dangerously so. Slavery proved as injurious to her as it did to me. When I went there, she was a pious, warm, and tender-hearted woman. There was no sorrow or suffering for which she had not a tear. She had bread for the hungry, clothes for the naked, and comfort for every mourner that came within her reach. Slavery soon proved its ability to divest her of these heavenly qualities. Under its influence, the tender heart became stone, and the lamblike disposition gave way to one of tiger-like fierceness. The first step in her downward course was in her ceasing to instruct me. She now commenced to practise her husband's precepts. She finally became even more violent in her opposition than her husband himself. She was not satisfied with simply doing as well as he had commanded; she seemed anxious to do better. Nothing seemed to make her more angry than to see me with a newspaper. She seemed to think that here lay the danger. I have had her rush at me with a face made all up of fury, and snatch from me a newspaper, in a manner that fully revealed her apprehension. She was an apt woman; and a little experience soon demonstrated, to her satisfaction, that education and slavery were incompatible with each other.

From this time I was most narrowly watched. If I was in a separate room any considerable length of time, I was sure to be suspected of having a book, and was at once called to give an account of myself. All this, however, was too late. The first step had been taken. Mistress, in teaching me the alphabet, had given me the *inch*, and no precaution could prevent me from taking the *ell*.

The plan which I adopted, and the one by which I was most successful, was that of making friends of all the little white boys whom I met in the street. As many of these as I could, I converted into teachers. With their kindly aid, obtained at different times and in different places, I finally succeeded in learning to read. When I was sent of errands, I always took my book with me, and by going one part of my errand quickly, I found time to get a lesson before my return. I used also to carry bread with me, enough of which was always in the house, and to which I was always welcome; for I was much better off in this regard than many of the poor white children in our neighborhood. This bread I used to bestow upon the hungry little urchins, who, in return, would give me that more valuable bread of knowledge. I am strongly tempted to give the names of two or three of those little boys, as a testimonial of the gratitude and affection I bear them; but prudence forbids;—not that it would injure me, but it might embarrass them; for it is almost an unpardonable offence to teach slaves to read in this Christian country. It is enough to say of the dear little fellows, that they lived on Philpot Street, very near Durgin and Bailey's ship-yard. I used to talk this matter of slavery over with them. I would sometimes say to them, I wished I could be as free as they would be when they got to be men. "You will be free as soon as you are twenty-one, but I am *a slave for life*! Have not I as good a right to be free as you have?"

These words used to trouble them; they would express for me the liveliest sympathy, and console me with the hope that something would occur by which I might be free.

I was now about twelve years old, and the thought of being *a slave for life* began to bear heavily upon my heart. Just about this time, I got hold of a book entitled "The Columbian Orator."[59] Every opportunity I got, I used

---

59. Reading *The Columbian Orator* ("Columbian" means "American" here) was a life-changing event for the young Frederick Douglass because it gave him access to the print-based world of white American children in early nineteenth-century America. By purchasing this book, Douglass gained entry to the world of formal education he was denied access to otherwise, as he could not attend public schools restricted to white students. Caleb Bingham's book (1797) had a subtitle that indicates its incredible range of topics: *The Columbian Orator: Containing a Variety of Original and Selected Pieces Together with Rules Calculated to Improve Youth and Others in the Ornamental and Useful Art of Eloquence*; the book included extracts from such figures as George Washington, Judah, Thomas Muir, Cato, Aesop, Benjamin Franklin, Joseph Addison, Christ, Lord Mansfield, and many others. The 1858 edition included an extract from Douglass's second version of his autobiography, *My Bondage and My Freedom*. At the age of twelve, when Douglass bought a used copy of Bingham's book, he was presented with a debate between a slave and a master, a debate that logically refuted the master's claim that slavery could be justified; Douglass would rely on logic as well as wit, sarcasm, and moral persuasion, in his numerous attacks on slavery when he became an abolitionist. Although Douglass mistakenly cites the English playwright Richard Brinsley Sheridan as the deliverer of a speech in support of Catholic Emancipation in Ireland, his point is valid: that is, that Arthur O'Connor's speech on Catholic Emancipation is similar to American eloquence when used to attack slavery; the link between freedom and literacy was emerging very clearly in Douglass's mind and imagination. The long-standing debate about whether literacy cut Douglass (and other black writers) off from their folk roots can also be glimpsed here, but it assumes a necessary contradiction between being literate and being authentically black. Literacy did cause problems for Douglass and his first wife Anna Murray Douglass.

to read this book. Among much of other interesting matter, I found in it a dialogue between a master and his slave. The slave was represented as having run away from his master three times. The dialogue represented the conversation which took place between them, when the slave was retaken the third time. In this dialogue, the whole argument in behalf of slavery was brought forward by the master, all of which was disposed of by the slave. The slave was made to say some very smart as well as impressive things in reply to his master—things which had the desired though unexpected effect; for the conversation resulted in the voluntary emancipation of the slave on the part of the master.

In the same book, I met with one of Sheridan's mighty speeches on and in behalf of Catholic emancipation. These were choice documents to me. I read them over and over again with unabated interest. They gave tongue to interesting thoughts of my own soul, which had frequently flashed through my mind, and died away for want of utterance. The moral which I gained from the dialogue was the power of truth over the conscience of even a slaveholder. What I got from Sheridan was a bold denunciation of slavery, and a powerful vindication of human rights. The reading of these documents enabled me to utter my thoughts, and to meet the arguments brought forward to sustain slavery; but while they relieved me of one difficulty, they brought on another even more painful than the one of which I was relieved. The more I read, the more I was led to abhor and detest my enslavers. I could regard them in no other light than a band of successful robbers, who had left their homes, and gone to Africa, and stolen us from our homes, and in a strange land reduced us to slavery. I loathed them as being the meanest as well as the most wicked of men. As I read and contemplated the subject, behold! that very discontentment which Master Hugh had predicted would follow my learning to read had already come, to torment and sting my soul to unutterable anguish. As I writhed under it, I would at times feel that learning to read had been a curse rather than a blessing. It had given me a view of my wretched condition, without the remedy. It opened my eyes to the horrible pit, but to no ladder upon which to get out. In moments of agony, I envied my fellow-slaves for their stupidity. I have often wished myself a beast. I preferred the condition of the meanest reptile to my own. Any thing, no matter what, to get rid of thinking! It was this everlasting thinking of my condition that tormented me. There was no getting rid of it. It was pressed upon me by every object within sight or hearing, animate or inanimate. The silver trump of freedom had roused my soul to eternal wakefulness. Freedom now appeared, to disappear no more forever. It was heard in every sound, and seen in every thing. It was ever present to torment me with a sense of my wretched condition. I saw nothing without seeing it, I heard nothing without hearing it, and felt nothing without feeling it. It looked from every star, it smiled in every calm, breathed in every wind, and moved in every storm.

I often found myself regretting my own existence, and wishing myself dead; and but for the hope of being free, I have no doubt but that I should have killed myself, or done something for which I should have been killed. While in this state of mind, I was eager to hear any one speak of slavery. I was a ready listener. Every little while, I could hear something about the abolitionists.[60] It was some time before I found what the word meant. It was always used in such connections as to make it an interesting word to me. If a slave ran away and succeeded in getting clear, or if a slave killed his master, set fire to a barn, or did any thing very wrong in the mind of a slaveholder, it was spoken of as the fruit of *abolition*. Hearing the word in this connection very often, I set about learning what it meant. The dictionary afforded me little or no help. I found it was "the act of abolishing;" but then I did not know what was to be abolished. Here I was perplexed. I did not dare to ask any one about its meaning, for I was satisfied that it was something they wanted me to know very little about. After a patient waiting, I got one of our city papers, containing an account of the number of petitions from the north, praying for the abolition of slavery in the District of Columbia, and of the slave trade between the States. From this time I understood the words *abolition* and *abolitionist*, and always drew near when that word was spoken, expecting to hear something of importance to myself and fellow-slaves. The light broke in upon me by degrees. I went one day down on the wharf of Mr. Waters; and seeing two Irishmen unloading a scow of stone, I went, unasked, and helped them. When we had finished, one of them came to me and asked me if I were a slave. I told him I was. He asked, "Are ye a slave for life?" I told him that I was. The good Irishman seemed to be deeply affected by the statement. He said to the other that it was a pity so fine a little fellow as myself should be a slave for life. He said it was a shame to hold me. They both advised me to run away to the north; that I should find friends there, and that I should be free. I pretended not to be interested in what they said, and treated them as if I did not understand them; for I feared they might be treacherous. White men have been known to encourage slaves to escape, and then, to get the reward, catch them and return them to their masters. I was afraid that these seemingly good men might use me so; but I nevertheless remembered their advice, and from that time I resolved to run away. I looked forward to a time at which it would be safe for me to escape. I was too young to think of

---

60. The word "abolitionists" would later prove to be one of the most important words in Douglass's vocabulary, for he devoted much of his life to the abolition of slavery, and after the Civil War, to the abolition of racial prejudice against black Americans. Dickson J. Preston points out that Douglass learned something about the meaning of the word "abolition" when he found a leaflet that mocked abolitionists by calling them "Bobolitionists" (*Young Frederick Douglass*, p. 101).

doing so immediately; besides, I wished to learn how to write, as I might have occasion to write my own pass. I consoled myself with the hope that I should one day find a good chance. Meanwhile, I would learn to write.

The idea as to how I might learn to write was suggested to me by being in Durgin and Bailey's ship-yard, and frequently seeing the ship carpenters, after hewing, and getting a piece of timber ready for use, write on the timber the name of that part of the ship for which it was intended. When a piece of timber was intended for the larboard side, it would be marked thus—"L." When a piece was for the starboard side, it would be marked thus—"S." A piece for the larboard side forward, would be marked thus—"L. F." When a piece was for starboard side forward, it would be marked thus—"S. F." For larboard aft, it would be marked thus—"L. A." For starboard aft, it would be marked thus—"S. A." I soon learned the names of these letters, and for what they were intended when placed upon a piece of timber in the ship-yard. I immediately commenced copying them, and in a short time was able to make the four letters named.[61] After that, when I met with any boy who I knew could write, I would tell him I could write as well as he. The next word would be, "I don't believe you. Let me see you try it." I would then make the letters which I had been so fortunate as to learn, and ask him to beat that. In this way I got a good many lessons in writing, which it is quite possible I should never have gotten in any other way. During this time, my copy-book was the board fence, brick wall, and pavement; my pen and ink was a lump of chalk. With these, I learned mainly how to write. I then commenced and continued copying the Italics in Webster's Spelling Book,[62] until I could

---

61. Even as a boy, Douglass already had internalized the importance of systematic effort, which he later explained in his speech on self-made men: "But another element of the secret of success demands a word. That element is order, systematic endeavor. We succeed, not alone by the laborious exertion of our faculties, be they small or great, but by the regular, thoughtful and systematic exercise of them. Order, the first law of heaven, is itself a power. The battle is nearly lost when your lines are in disorder. Regular, orderly and systematic effort which moves without friction and needless loss of time or power; which has a place for everything and everything in its place; which knows just where to begin, how to proceed and where to end, though marked by no extraordinary outlay of energy or activity, will work wonders, not only in the matter of accomplishment, but also in the in- crease of the ability of the individual. It will make the weak man strong and the strong man stronger; the simple man wise and the wise man, wiser, and will insure success by the power and influence that belong to habit. On the other hand, no matter what gifts and what aptitudes a man may possess; no matter though his mind be of the highest order and fitted for the noblest achievements; yet, without this systematic effort, his genius will only serve as a fire of shavings, soon in blaze and soon out." ("Self-Made Men," 1872)

62. Like *The Columbian Orator*, Noah Webster's handbook for spelling was a staple in American public schools throughout the nineteenth century. Douglass anticipated Malcolm X's copying of the dictionary while he was incarcerated. Both men realized the secret of white control and power could be mastered by almost anyone determined to do so.

make them all without looking on the book. By this time, my little Master Thomas had gone to school, and learned how to write, and had written over a number of copy-books. These had been brought home, and shown to some of our near neighbors, and then laid aside. My mistress used to go to class meeting at the Wilk Street meetinghouse every Monday afternoon, and leave me to take care of the house. When left thus, I used to spend the time in writing in the spaces left in Master Thomas's copy-book, copying what he had written. I continued to do this until I could write a hand very similar to that of Master Thomas. Thus, after a long, tedious effort for years, I finally succeeded in learning how to write.[63]

CHAPTER VIII

IN a very short time after I went to live at Baltimore, my old master's youngest son Richard died; and in about three years and six months after his death, my old master, Captain Anthony, died, leaving only his son, Andrew, and daughter, Lucretia, to share his estate. He died while on a visit to see his daughter at Hillsborough. Cut off thus unexpectedly, he left no will as to the disposal of his property. It was therefore necessary to have a valuation of the property, that it might be equally divided between Mrs. Lucretia and Master Andrew. I was immediately sent for, to be valued with the other property. Here again my feelings rose up in detestation of slavery. I had now a new conception of my degraded condition. Prior to this, I had become, if not insensible to my lot, at least partly so. I left Baltimore with a young heart overborne with sadness, and a soul full of apprehension. I took passage with Captain Rowe, in the schooner Wild Cat, and, after a sail of about twenty-four hours, I found myself near the place of my birth. I had now been absent from it almost, if not quite, five years. I, however, remembered the place very well. I was only about five years old when I left it, to go and live with my old master on Colonel Lloyd's plantation; so that I was now between ten and eleven years old.

We were all ranked together at the valuation. Men and women, old and young, married and single, were ranked with horses, sheep, and swine.

---

63. This is a good metaphor for what Douglass and countless other African Americans have done: fill in the blanks in white literary culture, which likes to think that it has completely marginalized black discourse, whereas the latter has always found ways to work itself into written white culture, which is what Douglass is doing in his *Narrative*. He does not, however, merely copy white writing; he puts a black spin on it in his own published work. The spin helps explain why African American influence on American culture in general has been out of proportion to the relatively small percentage of blacks in the general population.

There were horses and men, cattle and women, pigs and children, all holding the same rank in the scale of being, and were all subjected to the same narrow examination. Silvery-headed age and sprightly youth, maids and matrons, had to undergo the same indelicate inspection. At this moment, I saw more clearly than ever the brutalizing effects of slavery upon both slave and slaveholder.

After the valuation, then came the division. I have no language to express the high excitement and deep anxiety which were felt among us poor slaves during this time. Our fate for life was now to be decided. We had no more voice in that decision than the brutes among whom we were ranked. A single word from the white men was enough—against all our wishes, prayers, and entreaties—to sunder forever the dearest friends, dearest kindred, and strongest ties known to human beings. In addition to the pain of separation, there was the horrid dread of falling into the hands of Master Andrew. He was known to us all as being a most cruel wretch,—a common drunkard, who had, by his reckless mismanagement and profligate dissipation, already wasted a large portion of his father's property. We all felt that we might as well be sold at once to the Georgia traders, as to pass into his hands; for we knew that that would be our inevitable condition,—a condition held by us all in the utmost horror and dread.

I suffered more anxiety than most of my fellow-slaves. I had known what it was to be kindly treated; they had known nothing of the kind. They had seen little or nothing of the world. They were in very deed men and women of sorrow, and acquainted with grief. Their backs had been made familiar with the bloody lash, so that they had become callous; mine was yet tender; for while at Baltimore I got few whippings, and few slaves could boast of a kinder master and mistress than myself; and the thought of passing out of their hands into those of Master Andrew—a man who, but a few days before, to give me a sample of his bloody disposition, took my little brother by the throat, threw him on the ground, and with the heel of his boot stamped upon his head till the blood gushed from his nose and ears—was well calculated to make me anxious as to my fate. After he had committed this savage outrage upon my brother, he turned to me, and said that was the way he meant to serve me one of these days,—meaning, I suppose, when I came into his possession.

Thanks to a kind Providence, I fell to the portion of Mrs. Lucretia, and was sent immediately back to Baltimore, to live again in the family of Master Hugh. Their joy at my return equalled their sorrow at my departure. It was a glad day to me. I had escaped a worse than lion's jaws. I was absent from Baltimore, for the purpose of valuation and division, just about one month, and it seemed to have been six.

Very soon after my return to Baltimore, my mistress, Lucretia, died, leaving her husband and one child, Amanda; and in a very short time after her death, Master Andrew died. Now all the property of my old master, slaves included, was in the hands of strangers,—strangers who had had nothing to do with accumulating it. Not a slave was left free. All remained slaves, from the youngest to the oldest. If any one thing in my experience, more than another, served to deepen my conviction of the infernal character of slavery, and to fill me with unutterable loathing of slaveholders, it was their base ingratitude to my poor old grandmother. She had served my old master faithfully from youth to old age. She had been the source of all his wealth; she had peopled his plantation with slaves; she had become a great grandmother in his service. She had rocked him in infancy, attended him in childhood, served him through life, and at his death wiped from his icy brow the cold death-sweat, and closed his eyes forever. She was nevertheless left a slave—a slave for life—a slave in the hands of strangers; and in their hands she saw her children, her grandchildren, and her great-grandchildren, divided, like so many sheep, without being gratified with the small privilege of a single word, as to their or her own destiny. And, to cap the climax of their base ingratitude and fiendish barbarity, my grandmother, who was now very old, having outlived my old master and all his children, having seen the beginning and end of all of them, and her present owners finding she was of but little value, her frame already racked with the pains of old age, and complete helplessness fast stealing over her once active limbs, they took her to the woods, built her a little hut, put up a little mud-chimney, and then made her welcome to the privilege of supporting herself there in perfect loneliness; thus virtually turning her out to die! If my poor old grandmother now lives,[64] she lives to suffer in utter loneliness; she lives to remember and mourn over the loss of children, the loss of grandchildren, and the loss of great-grandchildren. They are, in the language of the slave's poet, Whittier,—

"Gone, gone, sold and gone
To the rice swamp dank and lone,
Where the slave-whip ceaseless swings,
Where the noisome insect stings,
Where the fever-demon strews
Poison with the falling dews,

---

64. But, according to Preston:

In a . . . letter to Auld, published in the *North Star*, September 7, 1849, Douglass apologized for some of his earlier statements, admitting that he had been "unjust and unkind." Regarding his grandmother, Douglass had been informed "that you have taken her from the desolate hut, in which she formerly lived, into your own kitchen, and are providing for her in a manner becoming a gentleman and a Christian." However, the apology, as usual, never caught up with the accusation. Douglass permitted the 1848 letter to be reprinted in the appendix of his *Bondage and Freedom* (1855) without correction; and Auld did not even know of the 1849 letter when they met at St. Michaels in 1877. (Preston, p. 229, note 10)

Where the sickly sunbeams glare
Through the hot and misty air:—
Gone, gone, sold and gone
To the rice swamp dank and lone,
From Virginia hills and waters—
Woe is me, my stolen daughters!"[65]

The hearth is desolate. The children, the unconscious children, who once sang and danced in her presence, are gone. She gropes her way, in the darkness of age, for a drink of water. Instead of the voices of her children, she hears by day the moans of the dove, and by night the screams of the hideous owl. All is gloom. The grave is at the door. And now, when weighed down by the pains and aches of old age, when the head inclines to the feet, when the beginning and ending of human existence meet, and helpless infancy and painful old age combine together—at this time, this most needful time, the time for the exercise of that tenderness and affection which children only can exercise towards a declining parent—my poor old grandmother, the devoted mother of twelve children, is left all alone, in yonder little hut, before a few dim embers. She stands—she sits—she staggers—she falls—she groans—she dies—and there are none of her children or grandchildren present, to wipe from her wrinkled brow the cold sweat of death, or to place beneath the sod her fallen remains. Will not a righteous God visit for these things?[66]

In about two years after the death of Mrs. Lucretia, Master Thomas married his second wife. Her name was Rowena Hamilton. She was the eldest daughter of Mr. William Hamilton. Master now lived in St. Michael's. Not long after his marriage, a misunderstanding took place between himself and Master Hugh; and as a means of punishing his brother, he took me from him to live with himself at St. Michael's. Here I underwent another most painful separation. It, however, was not so severe as the one I dreaded at the division of property; for, during this interval, a great change had taken place in Master Hugh and his once kind and affectionate wife. The influence of brandy upon him, and of slavery upon her, had effected a disastrous change in the characters of both; so that, as far as they were concerned, I thought I had little to lose by the change. But it was not to them that I was attached. It

---

65. From John Greenleaf Whittier's "The Farewell of a Virginia Slave Mother to Her Daughters, Sold into Southern Bondage." Whittier was a white abolitionist.

66. Many American writers on both sides of the Mason-Dixon line interpreted the Civil War as divine retribution for the sin of slavery. Lincoln's second inaugural address includes the vivid line, "every drop of blood drawn with the lash, shall be paid by another drawn by the sword." Douglass was disgusted by institutionalized Christianity in the South but endorsed the spirit of it as he understood it.

was to those little Baltimore boys that I felt the strongest attachment. I had received many good lessons from them, and was still receiving them, and the thought of leaving them was painful indeed. I was leaving, too, without the hope of ever being allowed to return. Master Thomas had said he would never let me return again. The barrier betwixt himself and brother he considered impassable.

I then had to regret that I did not at least make the attempt to carry out my resolution to run away; for the chances of success are tenfold greater from the city than from the country.

I sailed from Baltimore for St. Michael's in the sloop Amanda, Captain Edward Dodson. On my passage, I paid particular attention to the direction which the steamboats took to go to Philadelphia. I found, instead of going down, on reaching North Point they went up the bay, in a northeasterly direction. I deemed this knowledge of the utmost importance. My determination to run away was again revived. I resolved to wait only so long as the offering of a favorable opportunity. When that came, I was determined to be off.

CHAPTER IX

I have now reached a period of my life when I can give dates. I left Baltimore, and went to live with Master Thomas Auld, at St. Michael's, in March, 1832. It was now more than seven years since I lived with him in the family of my old master, on Colonel Lloyd's plantation. We of course were now almost entire strangers to each other. He was to me a new master, and I to him a new slave. I was ignorant of his temper and disposition; he was equally so of mine. A very short time, however, brought us into full acquaintance with each other. I was made acquainted with his wife not less than with himself. They were well matched, being equally mean and cruel. I was now, for the first time during a space of more than seven years, made to feel the painful gnawings of hunger—a something which I had not experienced before since I left Colonel Lloyd's plantation. It went hard enough with me then, when I could look back to no period at which I had enjoyed a sufficiency. It was tenfold harder after living in Master Hugh's family, where I had always had enough to eat, and of that which was good. I have said Master Thomas was a mean man. He was so. Not to give a slave enough to eat, is regarded as the most aggravated development of meanness even among slaveholders. The rule is, no matter how coarse the food, only let there be enough of it. This is the theory; and in the part of Maryland from which I came, it is the general practice,—though there are many exceptions. Master Thomas gave us enough of neither coarse nor fine food. There were four slaves of us in the kitchen—my sister Eliza, my aunt Priscilla, Henny,[67] and myself; and we were allowed less than a half of a bushel of corn-meal per week, and very little else, either in the shape of meat or vegetables. It was not enough for us to subsist upon. We were therefore reduced to the wretched necessity of living at the expense of our neighbors. This we did by begging and stealing, whichever came handy in the time of need, the one being considered as legitimate as the other. A great many times have we poor creatures been nearly perishing with hunger, when food in abundance lay mouldering in the safe and smoke-house, and our pious mistress was aware of the fact; and yet that mistress and her husband would kneel every morning, and pray that God would bless them in basket and store!

Bad as all slaveholders are, we seldom meet one destitute of every element of character commanding respect. My master was one of this rare sort. I do not know of one single noble act ever performed by him. The leading trait in his character was meanness; and if there were any other element in his nature, it was made subject to this. He was mean; and, like most other mean men, he lacked the ability to conceal his meanness. Captain Auld was not born a slaveholder. He had been a poor man, master only of a Bay craft. He came into possession of all his slaves by marriage; and of all men, adopted slaveholders are the worst. He was cruel, but cowardly. He commanded without firmness. In the enforcement of his rules, he was at times rigid, and at times lax. At times, he spoke to his slaves with the firmness of Napoleon[68] and the fury of a demon; at other times, he might well be mistaken for an inquirer who had lost his way. He did nothing of himself. He might have passed for a lion, but for his ears. In all things noble which he attempted, his own meanness shone most conspicuous. His airs, words, and actions, were the airs, words, and actions of born slaveholders, and, being assumed, were awkward enough. He was not even a good imitator. He possessed all the disposition to deceive, but wanted the power. Having no resources within himself, he was compelled to be the copyist of many, and being such, he was forever the victim of inconsistency; and of consequence he was an object of contempt, and was held as such even by his slaves. The luxury of having slaves of his own to wait upon him was something new and unprepared for. He was a slaveholder without the ability to hold slaves. He found himself incapable of managing his slaves either by force, fear, or fraud. We seldom called him "master;" we generally called him "Captain Auld," and were hardly disposed to title him at all. I doubt not that our conduct had much to do with making him appear awkward, and of consequence fretful. Our want of reverence for

---

67. Douglass's cousin.
68. Famous nineteenth-century French general and Emperor of France.

him must have perplexed him greatly. He wished to have us call him master, but lacked the firmness necessary to command us to do so. His wife used to insist upon our calling him so, but to no purpose. In August, 1832, my master attended a Methodist camp-meeting held in the Bay-side, Talbot county, and there experienced religion. I indulged a faint hope that his conversion would lead him to emancipate his slaves, and that, if he did not do this, it would, at any rate, make him more kind and humane. I was disappointed in both these respects. It neither made him to be humane to his slaves, nor to emancipate them. If it had any effect on his character, it made him more cruel and hateful in all his ways; for I believe him to have been a much worse man after his conversion than before. Prior to his conversion, he relied upon his own depravity to shield and sustain him in his savage barbarity; but after his conversion, he found religious sanction and support for his slaveholding cruelty. He made the greatest pretensions to piety. His house was the house of prayer. He prayed morning, noon, and night. He very soon distinguished himself among his brethren, and was soon made a class-leader and exhorter. His activity in revivals was great, and he proved himself an instrument in the hands of the church in converting many souls. His house was the preachers' home. They used to take great pleasure in coming there to put up; for while he starved us, he stuffed them. We have had three or four preachers there at a time. The names of those who used to come most frequently while I lived there, were Mr. Storks, Mr. Ewery, Mr. Humphry, and Mr. Hickey. I have also seen Mr. George Cookman at our house. We slaves loved Mr. Cookman. We believed him to be a good man. We thought him instrumental in getting Mr. Samuel Harrison, a very rich slaveholder, to emancipate his slaves; and by some means got the impression that he was laboring to effect the emancipation of all the slaves. When he was at our house, we were sure to be called in to prayers. When the others were there, we were sometimes called in and sometimes not. Mr. Cookman took more notice of us than either of the other ministers. He could not come among us without betraying his sympathy for us, and, stupid as we were, we had the sagacity to see it.

While I lived with my master in St. Michael's, there was a white young man, a Mr. Wilson, who proposed to keep a Sabbath school for the instruction of such slaves as might be disposed to learn to read the New Testament. We met but three times, when Mr. West and Mr. Fairbanks, both class-leaders, with many others, came upon us with sticks and other missiles, drove us off, and forbade us to meet again. Thus ended our little Sabbath school in the pious town of St. Michael's.

I have said my master found religious sanction for his cruelty. As an example, I will state one of many facts going to prove the charge. I have seen him tie up a lame young woman, and whip her with a heavy cowskin upon her naked shoulders, causing the warm red blood to drip; and, in justification of the bloody deed, he would quote this passage of Scripture—"He that knoweth his master's will, and doeth it not, shall be beaten with many stripes."[69]

Master would keep this lacerated young woman tied up in this horrid situation four or five hours at a time. I have known him to tie her up early in the morning, and whip her before breakfast; leave her, go to his store, return at dinner, and whip her again, cutting her in the places already made raw with his cruel lash. The secret of master's cruelty toward "Henny" is found in the fact of her being almost helpless. When quite a child, she fell into the fire, and burned herself horribly. Her hands were so burnt that she never got the use of them. She could do very little but bear heavy burdens. She was to master a bill of expense; and as he was a mean man, she was a constant offence to him. He seemed desirous of getting the poor girl out of existence. He gave her away once to his sister; but, being a poor gift, she was not disposed to keep her. Finally, my benevolent master, to use his own words, "set her adrift to take care of herself." Here was a recently-converted man, holding on upon the mother, and at the same time turning out her helpless child, to starve and die! Master Thomas was one of the many pious slaveholders who hold slaves for the very charitable purpose of taking care of them.

My master and myself had quite a number of differences. He found me unsuitable to his purpose. My city life, he said, had had a very pernicious effect upon me. It had almost ruined me for every good purpose, and fitted me for every thing which was bad. One of my greatest faults was that of letting his horse run away, and go down to his father-in-law's farm, which was about five miles from St. Michael's. I would then have to go after it. My reason for this kind of carelessness, or carefulness, was, that I could always get something to eat when I went there. Master William Hamilton, my master's father-in-law, always gave his slaves enough to eat. I never left there hungry, no matter how great the need of my speedy return. Master Thomas at length said he would stand it no longer. I had lived with him nine months, during which time he had given me a number of severe whippings, all to no good purpose. He resolved to put me out, as he said, to be broken; and, for this purpose, he let me for one year to a man named Edward Covey. Mr. Covey was a poor man, a farm-renter. He rented the place upon which he lived, as also the hands with which he tilled it. Mr. Covey had acquired a very high reputation for breaking young slaves, and this reputation was of immense value to him. It enabled him to get his farm tilled with much less expense to himself than he could have had it done without such a reputation. Some slaveholders thought it not much loss to allow Mr. Covey to have their slaves one year, for the sake of the training to which they were subjected, without any other compensation. He could hire young help with

---

69. Luke 12:47.

great ease, in consequence of this reputation. Added to the natural good qualities of Mr. Covey, he was a professor of religion—a pious soul—a member and a class-leader in the Methodist church. All of this added weight to his reputation as a "nigger-breaker." I was aware of all the facts, having been made acquainted with them by a young man who had lived there. I nevertheless made the change gladly; for I was sure of getting enough to eat, which is not the smallest consideration to a hungry man.

CHAPTER X[70]

I had left Master Thomas's house, and went to live with Mr. Covey, on the 1st of January, 1833. I was now, for the first time in my life, a field hand. In my new employment, I found myself even more awkward than a country boy appeared to be in a large city. I had been at my new home but one week before Mr. Covey gave me a very severe whipping, cutting my back, causing the blood to run, and raising ridges on my flesh as large as my little finger. The details of this affair are as follows: Mr. Covey sent me, very early in the morning of one of our coldest days in the month of January, to the woods, to get a load of wood. He gave me a team of unbroken oxen. He told me which was the in-hand ox, and which the off-hand one.[71] He then tied the end of a large rope around the horns of the in-hand ox, and gave me the other end of it, and told me, if the oxen started to run, that I must hold on upon the rope. I had never driven oxen before, and of course I was very awkward. I, however, succeeded in getting to the edge of the woods with little difficulty; but I had got a very few rods into the

---

70. The most frequently anthologized and famous chapter in the *Narrative*, mainly because it dramatized Douglass's victory over the slavebreaker, Edward Covey. Douglass implies that standing up to and defeating evil is sometimes the only recourse in vanquishing evil; in this may lie the seed of his later rejection of the Garrisonians because they were pacifists and did not seem to understand that there was no alternative to violence if slavery was to be abolished. Even though Garrison's influence on the *Narrative* is considerable, Douglass resists it in direct and indirect ways. This chapter is also in the mainstream of traditional presentations of heroism in American culture: a single individual male defeats another one in physical combat; by implication endorsing this model, Douglass gained the respect and admiration of many readers, particularly male readers in 1845 and ever since. One of the biggest costs in this model of heroism is that it excludes women, in particular Douglass's Aunt Hester, from the category of heroism by abandoning them to the category of passive victims. Women are an absence on this map, but there are other ways of conceiving heroism that foreground women, as Harriet Jacobs made clear in *Incidents in the Life of a Slave Girl* (1861).

71. The off-hand ox would be the ox on the right; the in-hand one would be the ox on the left.

woods, when the oxen took fright, and started full tilt, carrying the cart against trees, and over stumps, in the most frightful manner. I expected every moment that my brains would be dashed out against the trees. After running thus for a considerable distance, they finally upset the cart, dashing it with great force against a tree, and threw themselves into a dense thicket. How I escaped death, I do not know. There I was, entirely alone, in a thick wood, in a place new to me. My cart was upset and shattered, my oxen were entangled among the young trees, and there was none to help me. After a long spell of effort, I succeeded in getting my cart righted, my oxen disentangled, and again yoked to the cart. I now proceeded with my team to the place where I had, the day before, been chopping wood, and loaded my cart pretty heavily, thinking in this way to tame my oxen. I then proceeded on my way home. I had now consumed one half of the day. I got out of the woods safely, and now felt out of danger. I stopped my oxen to open the woods gate; and just as I did so, before I could get hold of my ox-rope, the oxen again started, rushed through the gate, catching it between the wheel and the body of the cart, tearing it to pieces, and coming within a few inches of crushing me against the gate-post. Thus twice, in one short day, I escaped death by the merest chance. On my return, I told Mr. Covey what had happened, and how it happened. He ordered me to return to the woods again immediately. I did so, and he followed on after me. Just as I got into the woods, he came up and told me to stop my cart, and that he would teach me how to trifle away my time, and break gates. He then went to a large gum-tree, and with his axe cut three large switches, and, after trimming them up neatly with his pocketknife, he ordered me to take off my clothes. I made him no answer, but stood with my clothes on. He repeated his order. I still made him no answer, nor did I move to strip myself. Upon this he rushed at me with the fierceness of a tiger, tore off my clothes, and lashed me till he had worn out his switches, cutting me so savagely as to leave the marks visible for a long time after. This whipping was the first of a number just like it, and for similar offences.

I lived with Mr. Covey[72] one year. During the first six months, of that year, scarce a week passed without his whipping me. I was seldom free

---

72. Jack Williams, a character in *The Heroic Slave*, throws light on Mr. Covey, who would have liked to have been an overseer of Williams's ilk (Williams himself may have been based, at least in part, on a real overseer named William H. Merritt). Scoffing at what he considers to be the pathetic efforts of putting down the slave rebellion on the Creole, Williams says:

"Well, betwixt you and me," said Williams, "that whole affair on board of the Creole was miserably and disgracefully managed. Those black rascals got the upper hand of ye altogether; and, in my opinion, the whole disaster was the result of ignorance of the real character of darkies in general. With half a dozen resolute white men, (I say it not boastingly,) from a sore back. My awkwardness was almost always his excuse for whipping me. We were worked fully up to the point of endurance. Long before day we were up, our horses fed, and by the first approach of day we were off to the field with our hoes and ploughing teams. Mr. Covey gave us enough to eat, but scarce time to eat it. We were often less than five minutes taking our meals. We were often in the field from the first approach of day till its last lingering ray had left us; and at saving-fodder time, midnight often caught us in the field binding blades.[73]

Covey would be out with us. The way he used to stand it, was this. He would spend the most of his afternoons in bed. He would then come out fresh in the evening, ready to urge us on with his words, example, and frequently with the whip. Mr. Covey was one of the few slaveholders who could and did work with his hands. He was a hard-working man. He knew by himself just what a man or a boy could do. There was no deceiving him. His work went on in his absence almost as well as in his presence; and he had the faculty of making us feel that he was ever present with us. This he did by surprising us. He seldom approached the spot where we were at work openly, if he could do it secretly. He always aimed at taking us by surprise. Such was his cunning, that we used to call him, among ourselves, "the snake." When we were at work in the cornfield, he would sometimes crawl on his hands and knees to avoid detection, and all at once he would rise nearly in our midst, and scream out, "Ha, ha! Come, come! Dash on, dash on!" This being his mode of attack, it was never safe to stop a single minute. His comings were like a thief in the night.[74] He appeared to us as being ever at hand. He was under every tree, behind every stump, in every bush, and at every window, on the plantation. He would sometimes mount

---

I could have had the rascals in irons in ten minutes, not because I'm so strong, but I know how to manage 'em. With my back against the caboose, I could, myself, have flogged a dozen of them; and had I been on board, by every monster of the deep, every black devil of 'em all would have had his neck stretched from the yard-arm. Ye made a mistake in yer manner of fighting 'em. All that is needed in dealing with a set of rebellious darkies, is to show that yer not afraid of 'em. For my own part, I would not honor a dozen niggers by pointing a gun at one on 'em,—a good stout whip, or a stiff rope's end, is better than all the guns at Old Point to quell a nigger insurrection. Why, sir, to take a gun to a nigger is the best way you can select to tell him you are afraid of him, and the best way of inviting his attack."

73. "Saving-fodder time" refers to harvest time, "blades" to blades of wheat.

74. I Thessalonians 5:2 and elsewhere in the Bible. This and the many other biblical quotations in the *Narrative* indicate to Douglass's readers that he is one of them in his familiarity with the Bible, but there is also a powerful irony in that Douglass suggests Covey, rather than being the Second Coming, was a snake ("coiled up in the corner of the wood-fence"), a diabolical suggestion. Covey did seem godlike to Douglass and his fellow slaves because he seemed to be everywhere; Douglass may be hinting that if people seem godlike, they are in effect.

his horse, as if bound to St. Michael's, a distance of seven miles, and in half an hour afterwards you would see him coiled up in the corner of the wood-fence, watching every motion of the slaves. He would, for this purpose, leave his horse tied up in the woods. Again, he would sometimes walk up to us, and give us orders as though he was upon the point of starting on a long journey, turn his back upon us, and make as though he was going to the house to get ready; and, before he would get half way thither, he would turn short and crawl into a fence-corner, or behind some tree, and there watch us till the going down of the sun.

Mr. Covey's *forte* consisted in his power to deceive. His life was devoted to planning and perpetrating the grossest deceptions. Every thing he possessed in the shape of learning or religion, he made conform to his disposition to deceive. He seemed to think himself equal to deceiving the Almighty. He would make a short prayer in the morning, and a long prayer at night; and, strange as it may seem, few men would at times appear more devotional than he. The exercises of his family devotions were always commenced with singing; and, as he was a very poor singer himself, the duty of raising the hymn generally came upon me. He would read his hymn, and nod at me to commence. I would at times do so; at others, I would not. My non-compliance would almost always produce much confusion. To show himself independent of me, he would start and stagger through with his hymn in the most discordant manner. In this state of mind, he prayed with more than ordinary spirit. Poor man! such was his disposition, and success at deceiving, I do verily believe that he sometimes deceived himself into the solemn belief, that he was a sincere worshipper of the most high God; and this, too, at a time when he may be said to have been guilty of compelling his woman slave to commit the sin of adultery. The facts in the case are these: Mr. Covey was a poor man; he was just commencing in life; he was only able to buy one slave; and, shocking as is the fact, he bought her, as he said, for a breeder.[75] This woman was named Caroline. Mr. Covey bought her from Mr. Thomas Lowe, about six miles from St. Michael's. She was a large, able-bodied woman, about twenty years old. She had already given birth to one child, which proved her to be just what he wanted. After buying her, he hired a married man of Mr. Samuel Harrison, to live with him one year; and him he used to fasten up with her every night! The result was, that, at the end of the year, the miserable woman gave birth to twins. At this result Mr. Covey seemed to be

---

75. The concept of the black woman as a breeder has led to one of the most outrageous stereotypes about black women in the white imagination: that they are just "naturally" sexual creatures and cannot be raped, as they are incapable of resistance. This lie, combined with the understandable silence of some black women subjected to white male sexual exploitation, has had catastrophic results.

highly pleased, both with the man and the wretched woman. Such was his joy, and that of his wife, that nothing they could do for Caroline during her confinement was too good, or too hard, to be done. The children were regarded as being quite an addition to his wealth.

If at any one time of my life more than another, I was made to drink the bitterest dregs of slavery, that time was during the first six months of my stay with Mr. Covey. We were worked in all weathers. It was never too hot or too cold; it could never rain, blow, hail, or snow, too hard for us to work in the field. Work, work, work, was scarcely more the order of the day than of the night. The longest days were too short for him, and the shortest nights too long for him. I was somewhat unmanageable when I first went there, but a few months of this discipline tamed me. Mr. Covey succeeded in breaking me. I was broken in body, soul, and spirit. My natural elasticity was crushed, my intellect languished, the disposition to read departed, the cheerful spark that lingered about my eye died; the dark night of slavery closed in upon me; and behold a man transformed into a brute![76]

Sunday was my only leisure time. I spent this in a sort of beast-like stupor, between sleep and wake, under some large tree. At times I would rise up, a flash of energetic freedom would dart through my soul, accompanied with a faint beam of hope, that flickered for a moment, and then vanished. I sank down again, mourning over my wretched condition. I was sometimes prompted to take my life, and that of Covey, but was prevented by a combination of hope and fear. My sufferings on this plantation seem now like a dream rather than a stern reality.

Our house stood within a few rods of the Chesapeake Bay, whose broad bosom was ever white with sails from every quarter of the habitable globe. Those beautiful vessels, robed in purest white, so delightful to the eye of freemen, were to me so many shrouded ghosts, to terrify and torment me with thoughts of my wretched condition. I have often, in the deep stillness of a summer's Sabbath, stood all alone upon the lofty banks of that noble bay, and traced, with saddened heart and tearful eye, the countless number of sails moving off to the mighty ocean. The sight of these always affected me powerfully. My thoughts would compel utterance; and there, with no audience but the Almighty, I would pour out my soul's complaint, in my rude way, with an apostrophe to the moving multitude of ships:—[77]

---

76. Douglass's implication, though, is that for Covey to turn Douglass into a brute, the former himself had to be one. And, indeed, for slavery to work, whites had to become what they claimed blacks were, and yet blacks were supposedly the problem.

77. The rhapsodic passage about ships in the Chesapeake Bay is one of the most moving in the *Narrative*; little did Douglass know at this time that he would later work as a ship calker.

"You are loosed from your moorings, and are free; I am fast in my chains, and am a slave! You move merrily before the gentle gale, and I sadly before the bloody whip! You are freedom's swift-winged angels, that fly round the world; I am confined in bands of iron! O that I were free! O, that I were on one of your gallant decks, and under your protecting wing! Alas! betwixt me and you, the turbid waters roll. Go on, go on. O that I could also go! Could I but swim! If I could fly! O, why was I born a man, of whom to make a brute! The glad ship is gone; she hides in the dim distance. I am left in the hottest hell of unending slavery. O God, save me! God, deliver me! Let me be free! Is there any God? Why am I a slave? I will run away. I will not stand it. Get caught, or get clear, I'll try it. I had as well die with ague as the fever. I have only one life to lose. I had as well be killed running as die standing. Only think of it; one hundred miles straight north, and I am free! Try it? Yes! God helping me, I will. It cannot be that I shall live and die a slave. I will take to the water. This very bay shall yet bear me into freedom. The steamboats steered in a north-east course from North Point. I will do the same; and when I get to the head of the bay, I will turn my canoe adrift, and walk straight through Delaware into Pennsylvania. When I get there, I shall not be required to have a pass; I can travel without being disturbed. Let but the first opportunity offer, and, come what will, I am off. Meanwhile, I will try to bear up under the yoke. I am not the only slave in the world. Why should I fret? I can bear as much as any of them. Besides, I am but a boy, and all boys are bound to some one. It may be that my misery in slavery will only increase my happiness when I get free. There is a better day coming."

Thus I used to think, and thus I used to speak to myself; goaded almost to madness at one moment, and at the next reconciling myself to my wretched lot.

I have already intimated that my condition was much worse, during the first six months of my stay at Mr. Covey's, than in the last six.[78] The circumstances leading to the change in Mr. Covey's course toward me

---

78. This passage suggests that even as a young man, Douglass already had a conception that he was destined to be a self-made man, that he was already becoming what he defines as a self-made man in one of his most famous speeches, delivered many times, "The Self-Made Man," in which the term is defined in the following manner:

> On the first point I may say that, by the term "self-made men," I mean especially what, to the popular mind, the term least imports. Self-made men are the men who, under peculiar difficulties and without the ordinary helps of favoring circumstances, have attained knowledge, usefulness, power and position and have learned from themselves the best uses to which life can be put in this world, and in the exercises of these uses to build up worthy character. They are the men who owe little or nothing to birth, relationship, friendly surroundings; to wealth inherited or to early approved means of education; who are what they

form an epoch in my humble history. You have seen how a man was made a slave; you shall see how a slave was made a man.[79] On one of the hottest days of the month of August, 1833, Bill Smith, William Hughes, a slave named Eli, and myself, were engaged in fanning wheat. Hughes was clearing the fanned wheat from before the fan. Eli was turning, Smith

---

are, without the aid of any favoring conditions by which other men usually rise in the world and achieve great results. In fact they are the men who are not brought up but who are obliged to come up, not only without the voluntary assistance or friendly co-operation of society, but often in open and derisive defiance of all the efforts of society and the tendency of circumstances to repress, retard and keep them down. They are the men who, in a world of schools, academies, colleges and other institutions of learning, are often compelled by unfriendly circumstances to acquire their education elsewhere and, amidst unfavorable conditions, to hew out for themselves a way to success, and thus to become the architects of their own good fortunes. They are in a peculiar sense, indebted to themselves for themselves. If they have traveled far, they have made the road on which they have travelled. If they have ascended high, they have built their own ladder. From the depths of poverty such as these have often come. From the heartless pavements of large and crowded cities; barefooted, homeless, and friendless, they have come. From hunger, rags and destitution, they have come; motherless and fatherless, they have come, and may come. Flung overboard in the midnight storm on the broad and tempest-tossed ocean of life; left without ropes, planks, oars or life-preservers, they have bravely buffeted the frowning billows and have risen in safety and life where others, supplied with the best appliances for safety and success, have fainted, despaired and gone down forever.

Such men as these, whether found in one position or another, whether in the college or in the factory; whether professors or plowmen; whether Caucasian or Indian; whether Anglo-Saxon or Anglo-African, are self-made men and are entitled to a certain measure of respect for their success and for proving to the world the grandest possibilities of human nature, of whatever variety of race or color.

Though a man of this class need not claim to be a hero or to be worshiped as such, there is genuine heroism in his struggle and something of sublimity and glory in his triumph. Every instance of such success is an example and a help to humanity. It, better than any mere assertion, gives us assurance of the latent powers and resources of simple and un-aided manhood. It dignifies labor, honors application, lessens pain and depression, dispels gloom from the brow of the destitute and weariness from the heart of him about to faint, and enables man to take hold of the roughest and flintiest hardships incident to the battle of life, with a lighter heart, with higher hopes and a larger courage. ("Self-Made Men," 1872)

Frederick Douglass relied to a considerable extent on Frederick Douglass to get the upper hand over Mr. Covey, signifying to Douglass's black readers especially, that what happens to you is largely up to you; self-exertion is the way to become a self-made man (whereas so many white masters relied on their slaves instead of on themselves).

79. One of the most famous sentences in the *Narrative*, this one, a rhetorical gem, begs the question of what the word "man" means. One point about the term "man" that Douglass seems to understand is that whether someone is a man or not must be seen; consequently, the kind of manhood that Harriet Jacobs embodies in *Incidents in the Life of a Slave Girl* (she hides in a garret for seven years to at least be able to see her children) would not qualify. Douglass associates being a man with violence between males, so again, Jacobs does not qualify. But given nineteenth-century standards of male honor, if Douglass wants his readers to judge him to be a man, he has to conform to the definition of it that presides over his fight with Covey.

was feeding, and I was carrying wheat to the fan. The work was simple, requiring strength rather than intellect; yet, to one entirely unused to such work, it came very hard. About three o'clock of that day, I broke down; my strength failed me; I was seized with a violent aching of the head, attended with extreme dizziness; I trembled in every limb. Finding what was coming, I nerved myself up, feeling it would never do to stop work. I stood as long as I could stagger to the hopper with grain. When I could stand no longer, I fell, and felt as if held down by an immense weight. The fan of course stopped; every one had his own work to do; and no one could do the work of the other, and have his own go on at the same time.

Mr. Covey was at the house, about one hundred yards from the treading-yard where we were fanning. On hearing the fan stop, he left immediately, and came to the spot where we were. He hastily inquired what the matter was. Bill answered that I was sick, and there was no one to bring wheat to the fan. I had by this time crawled away under the side of the post and rail-fence by which the yard was enclosed, hoping to find relief by getting out of the sun. He then asked where I was. He was told by one of the hands. He came to the spot, and, after looking at me awhile, asked me what was the matter. I told him as well as I could, for I scarce had strength to speak. He then gave me a savage kick in the side, and told me to get up. I tried to do so, but fell back in the attempt. He gave me another kick, and again told me to rise. I again tried, and succeeded in gaining my feet; but, stooping to get the tub with which I was feeding the fan, I again staggered and fell. While down in this situation, Mr. Covey took up the hickory slat with which Hughes had been striking off the half-bushel measure, and with it gave me a heavy blow upon the head, making a large wound, and the blood ran freely; and with this again told me to get up. I made no effort to comply, having now made up my mind to let him do his worst. In a short time after receiving this blow, my head grew better. Mr. Covey had now left me to my fate. At this moment I resolved, for the first time, to go to my master, enter a complaint, and ask his protection. In order to do this, I must that afternoon walk seven miles; and this, under the circumstances, was truly a severe undertaking. I was exceedingly feeble; made so as much by the kicks and blows which I received, as by the severe fit of sickness to which I had been subjected. I, however, watched my chance, while Covey was looking in an opposite direction, and started for St. Michael's. I succeeded in getting a considerable distance on my way to the woods, when Covey discovered me, and called after me to come back, threatening what he would do if I did not come. I disregarded both his calls and his threats, and made my way to the woods as fast as my feeble state would allow; and thinking I might be overhauled by him if I kept the road, I walked through the woods, keeping far enough from the road to avoid detection, and near enough to prevent losing my way. I had not gone far before my little strength again failed me. I could go no farther. I fell down, and lay for a considerable time. The blood was yet oozing from the wound on my head. For a time I thought I should bleed to death; and think now that I should have done so, but that the blood so matted my hair as to stop the wound. After lying there about three quarters of an hour, I nerved myself up again, and started on my way, through bogs and briers, barefooted and bare-headed, tearing my feet sometimes at nearly every step; and after a journey of about seven miles, occupying some five hours to perform it, I arrived at master's store. I then presented an appearance enough to affect any but a heart of iron. From the crown of my head to my feet, I was covered with blood. My hair was all clotted with dust and blood; my shirt was stiff with blood. I suppose I looked like a man who had escaped a den of wild beasts, and barely escaped them. In this state I appeared before my master, hum-bly entreating him to interpose his authority for my protection. I told him all the circumstances as well as I could, and it seemed, as I spoke, at times to affect him. He would then walk the floor, and seek to justify Covey by saying he expected I deserved it. He asked me what I wanted. I told him, to let me get a new home; that as sure as I lived with Mr. Covey again, I should live with but to die with him; that Covey would surely kill me; he was in a fair way for it. Master Thomas ridiculed the idea that there was any danger of Mr. Covey's killing me, and said that he knew Mr. Covey; that he was a good man, and that he could not think of taking me from him; that, should he do so, he would lose the whole year's wages; that I be-longed to Mr. Covey for one year, and that I must go back to him, come what might; and that I must not trouble him with any more stories, or that he would himself *get hold of me*. After threatening me thus, he gave me a very large dose of salts, telling me that I might remain in St. Michael's that night, (it being quite late,) but that I must be off back to Mr. Covey's early in the morning; and that if I did not, he would *get hold of me*, which meant that he would whip me. I remained all night, and, according to his orders, I started off to Covey's in the morning, (Saturday morning,) wearied in body and broken in spirit. I got no supper that night, or breakfast that morning. I reached Covey's about nine o'clock; and just as I was getting over the fence that divided Mrs. Kemp's fields from ours, out ran Covey with his cowskin, to give me another whipping. Before he could reach me, I succeeded in getting to the cornfield; and as the corn was very high, it afforded me the means of hiding. He seemed very angry, and searched for me a long time. My behavior was altogether unaccountable. He finally gave up the chase, thinking, I suppose, that I must come home for some-thing to eat; he would give himself no further trouble in looking for me. I spent that day mostly in the woods, having the alternative before me,—to go home and be whipped to death, or stay in the woods and be starved to death. That night, I fell in with Sandy Jenkins, a slave with whom I was somewhat acquainted. Sandy had a free wife who lived about four miles from Mr. Covey's; and it being Saturday, he was on his way to see her. I told him my circumstances, and he very kindly invited me to go home with him. I went home with him, and talked this whole matter over, and got his advice as to what course it was best for me to pursue. I found Sandy an old adviser. He told me, with great solemnity, I must go back to Covey; but that before I went, I must go with him into another part of the woods, where there was a certain root,[80] which, if I would take some of it with me, carrying it *always on my right side*, would render it impossible for Mr. Covey, or any other white man, to whip me. He said he had carried it for years; and since he had done so, he had never received a blow, and never expected to while he carried it. I at first rejected the idea, that the simple carrying of a root in my pocket would have any such effect as he had said, and was not disposed to take it; but Sandy impressed the necessity with much earnestness, telling me it could do no harm, if it did no good. To please him, I at length took the root, and, according to his direction, carried it upon my right side. This was Sunday morning. I immediately started for home; and upon entering the yard gate, out came Mr. Covey on his way to meeting. He spoke to me very kindly, bade me drive the pigs from a lot near by, and passed on towards the church. Now, this singular conduct of Mr. Covey really made me begin to think that there was something in the root which Sandy had given me; and had it been on any other day than Sunday, I could have attributed the conduct to no other cause than the influence of that root; and as it was, I was half inclined to think the root to be something more than I at first had taken it to be. All went well till Monday morning. On this morning, the virtue of the root was fully tested. Long before daylight, I was called to go and rub, curry, and feed, the horses. I obeyed, and was glad to obey. But whilst thus engaged, whilst in the act of throwing down some blades from the loft, Mr. Covey entered the stable with a long rope; and just as I was half out of the loft, he caught hold of my legs, and was about tying me. As soon as I found what he was up to, I gave a sudden spring, and as I did so, he holding to my legs, I was brought sprawling on the stable floor. Mr. Covey seemed now to think he had me, and could do what he pleased; but at this moment—from whence came the spirit I don't know—I resolved to fight; and, suiting my action to the resolution, I seized Covey hard by the throat; and as I did so, I rose. He held on to me, and I to him. My resistance was so entirely unexpected that Covey seemed taken all aback. He trembled like a leaf. This gave me assurance, and I held him uneasy, causing the blood to run where I touched him with the ends of my fingers. Mr. Covey soon called out to Hughes for help. Hughes came, and, while Covey held me, attempted to tie my right hand.

---

80. Some slaves believed that a root could provide supernatural powers; an African survival, this tradition could sometimes increase the confidence of its possessor, and in a sense, work.

While he was in the act of doing so, I watched my chance, and gave him a heavy kick close under the ribs. This kick fairly sickened Hughes, so that he left me in the hands of Mr. Covey. This kick had the effect of not only weakening Hughes, but Covey also. When he saw Hughes bending over with pain, his courage quailed. He asked me if I meant to persist in my resistance. I told him I did, come what might; that he had used me like a brute for six months, and that I was determined to be used so no longer. With that, he strove to drag me to a stick that was lying just out of the stable door. He meant to knock me down. But just as he was leaning over to get the stick, I seized him with both hands by his collar, and brought him by a sudden snatch to the ground. By this time, Bill came. Covey called upon him for assistance. Bill wanted to know what he could do. Covey said, "Take hold of him, take hold of him!" Bill said his master hired him out to work, and not to help to whip me; so he left Covey and myself to fight our own battle out. We were at it for nearly two hours. Covey at length let me go, puffing and blowing at a great rate, saying that if I had not resisted, he would not have whipped me half so much. The truth was, that he had not whipped me at all. I considered him as getting entirely the worst end of the bargain; for he had drawn no blood from me, but I had from him. The whole six months afterwards, that I spent with Mr. Covey, he never laid the weight of his finger upon me in anger. He would occasionally say, he didn't want to get hold of me again. "No," thought I, "you need not; for you will come off worse than you did before."

This battle with Mr. Covey was the turning-point in my career as a slave. It rekindled the few expiring embers of freedom, and revived within me a sense of my own manhood. It recalled the departed self-confidence, and inspired me again with a determination to be free. The gratification afforded by the triumph was a full compensation for whatever else might follow, even death itself. He only can understand the deep satisfaction which I experienced, who has himself repelled by force the bloody arm of slavery. I felt as I never felt before. It was a glorious resurrection,[81] from the tomb of slavery, to the heaven of freedom. My long-crushed spirit rose, cowardice departed, bold defiance took its place; and I now resolved that, however long I might remain a slave in form, the day had passed forever when I could be a slave in fact. I did not hesitate to let it be known of me, that the white man who expected to succeed in whipping, must also succeed in killing me.

---

81. This racialization of Christianity is one example of many of how Douglass and many other African Americans have put a black spin on Western traditions, thereby having an influence on white American culture out of proportion to their numbers in the population: for slaves, the white Christian notion of hell would be the South; the white Christian notion of heaven, the North; pharaoh the master of a plantation. Such a strategy allowed slaves the chance to put black messages in white envelopes.

From this time I was never again what might be called fairly whipped, though I remained a slave four years afterwards. I had several fights, but was never whipped.[82]

It was for a long time a matter of surprise to me why Mr. Covey did not immediately have me taken by the constable to the whipping-post, and there regularly whipped for the crime of raising my hand against a white man in defence of myself. And the only explanation I can now think of does not entirely satisfy me; but such as it is, I will give it. Mr. Covey enjoyed the most unbounded reputation for being a first-rate overseer and negro-breaker. It was of considerable importance to him. That reputation was at stake; and had he sent me—a boy about sixteen years old—to the public whipping-post, his reputation would have been lost; so, to save his reputation, he suffered me to go unpunished.

My term of actual service to Mr. Edward Covey ended on Christmas day, 1833. The days between Christmas and New Year's day are allowed as holidays; and, accordingly, we were not required to perform any labor, more than to feed and take care of the stock. This time we regarded as our own, by the grace of our masters; and we therefore used or abused it nearly as we pleased. Those of us who had families at a distance, were generally allowed to spend the whole six days in their society. This time, however, was spent in various ways. The staid, sober, thinking and industrious ones of our number would employ themselves in making corn-brooms, mats, horse-collars, and baskets; and another class of us would spend the time in hunting opossums, hares, and coons. But by far the larger part engaged in such sports and merriments as playing ball, wrestling, running foot-races,[83]

---

82. Douglass's later admiration for Madison Washington (adumbrated in this fight with Covey) in *The Heroic Slave* is based partly on the former's realization that they were similar in some ways: "It seems that Madison, by that mesmeric power which is the invariable accompaniment of genius, had already won the confidence of the gang, and was a sort of general-in-chief among them" (*The Heroic Slave*, 217). Douglass obviously saw in Madison Washington a model for African American male heroism, or, in other words, a man like Frederick Douglass. A key difference, though, is that Madison Washington used violence to bring about the successful freeing of 130 African slaves on the *Creole*, but Douglass was not personally involved in the violent overthrow of slavery, as two of his sons were in the Civil War, and as John Brown was in his famous raid on Harpers Ferry in 1859 (Douglass, a friend of Brown's, declined the opportunity to take part in the raid, which ended when then Colonel Robert E. Lee led U.S. Marines in an attack on the raiders).

83. Douglass's disapproval of such activities persisted throughout his life, probably because he associated sports with the masters' encouraging slaves to use the brief periods when they were not required to work in activities that distracted them from concentrating on abolishing slavery. Years after Douglass wrote his 1845 *Narrative*, he said in a speech:

"I do not desire my lecture to become a sermon; but, were this allowable, I would rebuke the growing tendency to sport and pleasure. The time, money and strength devoted to these phantoms, would banish darkness and hunger from every hearthstone in our land.

fiddling, dancing, and drinking whisky; and this latter mode of spending the time was by far the most agreeable to the feelings of our masters. A slave who would work during the holidays was considered by our masters as scarcely deserving them. He was regarded as one who rejected the favor of his master. It was deemed a disgrace not to get drunk at Christmas; and he was regarded as lazy indeed, who had not provided himself with the necessary means, during the year, to get whisky enough to last him through Christmas.

From what I know of the effect of these holidays upon the slave, I believe them to be among the most effective means in the hands of the slaveholder in keeping down the spirit of insurrection. Were the slaveholders at once to abandon this practice, I have not the slightest doubt it would lead to an immediate insurrection among the slaves. These holidays serve as conductors, or safety-valves, to carry off the rebellious spirit of enslaved humanity. But for these, the slave would be forced up to the wildest desperation; and woe betide the slaveholder, the day he ventures to remove or hinder the operation of those conductors! I warn him that, in such an event, a spirit will go forth in their midst, more to be dreaded than the most appalling earthquake.

The holidays are part and parcel of the gross fraud, wrong, and inhumanity of slavery. They are professedly a custom established by the benevolence of the slaveholders; but I undertake to say, it is the result of selfishness, and one of the grossest frauds committed upon the downtrodden slave. They do not give the slaves this time because they would

---

Multitudes, unconscious of any controlling object in life, flit, like birds, from point to point; now here, now there; and so accomplish nothing, either here to there.

For pleasures are like poppies spread,
You seize the flower, its bloom is shed!
Or like the snow-falls in the river,
    A moment white—then melts forever;
    Or like the borealis race,
    That flit ere you can point their place;
    Or like the rainbow's lovely form
    Evanishing amid the storm.—

They know most of pleasure who seek it least, and they least who seek it most. The cushion is soft to him who sits on it but seldom. The men behind the chairs at Saratoga and Newport, get better dinners than the men in them. We cannot serve two masters. When here, we cannot be there. If we accept ease, we must part with appetite. A pound of feathers is as heavy as a pound of iron,—and about as hard, if you sit on it long enough. Music is delightful, but too much of it wounds the ear like the filing of a saw. The lounge, to the lazy, becomes like flint; and to him, the most savory dishes lose their flavor" ("Self-Made Men," 1872). What may seem heavy-handed moral condemnation to modern readers may have been due to Douglass's unconditional hatred of slavery.

not like to have their work during its continuance, but because they know it would be unsafe to deprive them of it. This will be seen by the fact, that the slaveholders like to have their slaves spend those days just in such a manner as to make them as glad of their ending as of their beginning. Their object seems to be, to disgust their slaves with freedom, by plunging them into the lowest depths of dissipation. For instance, the slaveholders not only like to see the slave drink of his own accord, but will adopt various plans to make him drunk. One plan is, to make bets on their slaves, as to who can drink the most whisky without getting drunk; and in this way they succeed in getting whole multitudes to drink to excess. Thus, when the slave asks for virtuous freedom, the cunning slaveholder, knowing his ignorance, cheats him with a dose of vicious dissipation, artfully labelled with the name of liberty. The most of us used to drink it down, and the result was just what might be supposed; many of us were led to think that there was little to choose between liberty and slavery. We felt, and very properly too, that we had almost as well be slaves to man as to rum. So, when the holidays ended, we staggered up from the filth of our wallowing, took a long breath, and marched to the field,—feeling, upon the whole, rather glad to go, from what our master had deceived us into a belief was freedom, back to the arms of slavery.

I have said that this mode of treatment is a part of the whole system of fraud and inhumanity of slavery. It is so. The mode here adopted to disgust the slave with freedom, by allowing him to see only the abuse of it, is carried out in other things. For instance, a slave loves molasses; he steals some. His master, in many cases, goes off to town, and buys a large quantity; he returns, takes his whip, and commands the slave to eat the molasses, until the poor fellow is made sick at the very mention of it. The same mode is sometimes adopted to make the slaves refrain from asking for more food than their regular allowance. A slave runs through his allowance, and applies for more. His master is enraged at him; but, not willing to send him off without food, gives him more than is necessary, and compels him to eat it within a given time. Then, if he complains that he cannot eat it, he is said to be satisfied neither full nor fasting, and is whipped for being hard to please! I have an abundance of such illustrations of the same principle, drawn from my own observation, but think the cases I have cited sufficient. The practice is a very common one.

On the first of January, 1834, I left Mr. Covey, and went to live with Mr. William Freeland, who lived about three miles from St. Michael's. I soon found Mr. Freeland a very different man from Mr. Covey. Though not rich, he was what would be called an educated southern gentleman. Mr. Covey, as I have shown, was a well-trained negro-breaker and slave-driver. The former (slaveholder though he was) seemed to possess some regard for honor, some reverence for justice, and some respect for humanity. The latter seemed totally insensible to all such sentiments. Mr. Freeland had many of the faults peculiar to slaveholders, such as being very passionate and fretful; but I must do him the justice to say, that he was exceedingly free from those degrading vices to which Mr. Covey was constantly addicted. The one was open and frank, and we always knew where to find him. The other was a most artful deceiver, and could be understood only by such as were skilful enough to detect his cunningly-devised frauds. Another advantage I gained in my new master was, he made no pretensions to, or profession of, religion; and this, in my opinion, was truly a great advantage. I assert most unhesitatingly, that the religion of the south is a mere covering for the most horrid crimes,—a justifier of the most appalling barbarity,—a sanctifier of the most hateful frauds,—and a dark shelter under, which the darkest, foulest, grossest, and most infernal deeds of slaveholders find the strongest protection. Were I to be again reduced to the chains of slavery, next to that enslavement, I should regard being the slave of a religious master[84] the greatest calamity that could befall me. For of all slaveholders with whom I have ever met, religious slaveholders are the worst. I have ever found them the meanest and basest, the most cruel and cowardly, of all others. It was my unhappy lot not only to belong to a religious slaveholder, but to live in a community of such religionists. Very near Mr. Freeland lived the Rev. Daniel Weeden, and in the same neighborhood lived the Rev. Rigby Hopkins. These were members and ministers in the Reformed Methodist Church. Mr. Weeden owned, among others, a woman slave, whose name I have forgotten. This woman's back, for weeks, was kept literally raw, made so by the lash of this merciless, religious wretch. He used to hire hands. His maxim was, Behave well or behave ill, it is the duty of a master occasionally to whip a slave, to remind him of his master's authority. Such was his theory, and such his practice.

Mr. Hopkins was even worse than Mr. Weeden. His chief boast was his ability to manage slaves. The peculiar feature of his government was that of whipping slaves in advance of deserving it. He always managed to have one or more of his slaves to whip every Monday morning. He did this to alarm their fears, and strike terror into those who escaped. His plan was to whip for the smallest offences, to prevent the commission of large ones.

---

84. Douglass despised institutionalized Christianity, which he distinguished from the Christianity of Christ. He saw white churches as hypocritical and contradictory because many would not allow black children to learn how to spell the word "God," and yet these same churches expected black children to be knowledgeable about the concept. On the other hand, the black churches Douglass was a part of allowed him to preach, which is connected to his career as an orator and abolitionist. Because black churches were the only institution black people have controlled in the United States until recently, it is no accident so many black leaders began their careers in them, from Douglass through more recent examples, such as Jesse Jackson, Dr. Martin Luther King Jr., and Reverend Al Sharpton.

Mr. Hopkins could always find some excuse for whipping a slave. It would astonish one, unaccustomed to a slaveholding life, to see with what wonderful ease a slaveholder can find things, of which to make occasion to whip a slave. A mere look, word, or motion,—a mistake, accident, or want of power,—are all matters for which a slave may be whipped at any time. Does a slave look dissatisfied? It is said, he has the devil in him, and it must be whipped out. Does he speak loudly when spoken to by his master? Then he is getting high-minded, and should be taken down a button-hole lower. Does he forget to pull off his hat at the approach of a white person? Then he is wanting in reverence, and should be whipped for it. Does he ever venture to vindicate his conduct, when censured for it? Then he is guilty of impudence,—one of the greatest crimes of which a slave can be guilty. Does he ever venture to suggest a different mode of doing things from that pointed out by his master? He is indeed presumptuous, and getting above himself; and nothing less than a flogging will do for him. Does he, while ploughing, break a plough,—or, while hoeing, break a hoe? It is owing to his carelessness, and for it a slave must always be whipped. Mr. Hopkins could always find something of this sort to justify the use of the lash, and he seldom failed to embrace such opportunities. There was not a man in the whole county, with whom the slaves who had the getting their own home, would not prefer to live, rather than with this Rev. Mr. Hopkins. And yet there was not a man any where round, who made higher professions of religion, or was more active in revivals,—more attentive to the class, love-feast, prayer and preaching meetings, or more devotional in his family,—that prayed earlier, later, louder, and longer,—than this same reverend slave-driver, Rigby Hopkins.

But to return to Mr. Freeland, and to my experience while in his employment. He, like Mr. Covey, gave us enough to eat; but, unlike Mr. Covey, he also gave us sufficient time to take our meals. He worked us hard, but always between sunrise and sunset. He required a good deal of work to be done, but gave us good tools with which to work. His farm was large, but he employed hands enough to work it, and with ease, compared with many of his neighbors. My treatment, while in his employment, was heavenly, compared with what I experienced at the hands of Mr. Edward Covey.

Mr. Freeland was himself the owner of but two slaves. Their names were Henry Harris and John Harris. The rest of his hands he hired. These consisted of myself, Sandy Jenkins,* and Handy Caldwell.

*This is the same man who gave me the roots to prevent my being whipped by Mr. Covey. He was "a clever soul." We used frequently to talk about the fight with Covey, and as often as we did so, he would claim my success as the result of the roots which he gave me. This superstition is very common among the more ignorant slaves. A slave seldom dies but that his death is attributed to trickery.

Henry and John were quite intelligent, and in a very little while after I went there, I succeeded in creating in them a strong desire to learn how to read. This desire soon sprang up in the others also. They very soon mustered up some old spelling-books, and nothing would do but that I must keep a Sabbath school. I agreed to do so, and accordingly devoted my Sundays to teaching these my loved fellow-slaves how to read. Neither of them knew his letters when I went there. Some of the slaves of the neighboring farms found what was going on, and also availed themselves of this little opportunity to learn to read. It was understood, among all who came, that there must be as little display about it as possible. It was necessary to keep our religious masters at St. Michael's unacquainted with the fact, that, instead of spending the Sabbath in wrestling, boxing, and drinking whisky, we were trying to learn how to read the will of God; for they had much rather see us engaged in those degrading sports, than to see us behaving like intellectual, moral, and accountable beings. My blood boils as I think of the bloody manner in which Messrs. Wright Fairbanks and Garrison West, both class-leaders, in connection with many others, rushed in upon us with sticks and stones, and broke up our virtuous little Sabbath school, at St. Michael's—all calling themselves Christians! humble followers of the Lord Jesus Christ! But I am again digressing.

I held my Sabbath school at the house of a free colored man, whose name I deem it imprudent to mention; for should it be known, it might embarrass him greatly, though the crime of holding the school was committed ten years ago. I had at one time over forty scholars, and those of the right sort, ardently desiring to learn. They were of all ages, though mostly men and women. I look back to those Sundays with an amount of pleasure not to be expressed. They were great days to my soul. The work of instructing my dear fellow-slaves was the sweetest engagement with which I was ever blessed. We loved each other, and to leave them at the close of the Sabbath was a severe cross indeed. When I think that these precious souls are to-day shut up in the prison-house of slavery, my feelings overcome me, and I am almost ready to ask, "Does a righteous God govern the universe? and for what does he hold the thunders in his right hand, if not to smite the oppressor, and deliver the spoiled out of the hand of the spoiler?" These dear souls came not to Sabbath school because it was popular to do so, nor did I teach them because it was reputable to be thus engaged. Every moment they spent in that school, they were liable to be taken up, and given thirty-nine lashes. They came because they wished to learn. Their minds had been starved by their cruel masters. They had been shut up in mental darkness. I taught them, because it was the delight of my soul to be doing something that looked like bettering the condition of my race. I kept up my school nearly the whole year I lived with Mr. Freeland; and, beside my Sabbath school, I devoted three evenings in the week, during the winter, to teaching the slaves at home. And I have the happiness to know, that several of those who came to Sabbath school learned how to read; and that one, at least, is now free through my agency.

The year passed off smoothly. It seemed only about half as long as the year which preceded it. I went through it without receiving a single blow. I will give Mr. Freeland the credit of being the best master I ever had, *till I became my own master*. For the ease with which I passed the year, I was, however, somewhat indebted to the society of my fellow-slaves. They were noble souls; they not only possessed loving hearts, but brave ones. We were linked and interlinked with each other. I loved them with a love stronger than any thing I have experienced since. It is sometimes said that we slaves do not love and confide in each other. In answer to this assertion, I can say, I never loved any or confided in any people more than my fellow-slaves, and especially those with whom I lived at Mr. Freeland's. I believe we would have died for each other. We never undertook to do any thing, of any importance, without a mutual consultation. We never moved separately. We were one; and as much so by our tempers and dispositions, as by the mutual hardships to which we were necessarily subjected by our condition as slaves.[85]

At the close of the year 1834, Mr. Freeland again hired me of my master, for the year 1835. But, by this time, I began to want to live *upon free land* as well as *with Freeland*; and I was no longer content, therefore, to live with him or any other slaveholder. I began, with the commencement of the year, to prepare myself for a final struggle, which should decide my fate one way or the other. My tendency was upward. I was fast approaching manhood, and year after year had passed, and I was still a slave. These thoughts roused me—I must do something. I therefore resolved that 1835 should not pass without witnessing an attempt, on my part, to secure my liberty. But I was not willing to cherish this determination alone. My fellow-slaves were dear to me. I was anxious to have them participate with me in this, my life-giving determination. I therefore, though with great prudence, commenced early to ascertain their views and feelings in regard to their condition, and to imbue their minds with thoughts of freedom. I bent myself to devising ways and means for our escape, and meanwhile strove, on all fitting occasions, to impress them with the gross fraud and inhumanity of slavery. I went first to Henry, next to John, then to the others. I found, in them all, warm hearts and noble spirits. They were ready to hear, and ready to act when a feasible plan should be proposed. This was what I wanted. I talked to them of our want of manhood, if we submitted

---

85. The importance of black friends to Douglass cannot be overestimated; he was always looking for camaraderie among black, and sometimes, white people; this need challenges the image of him as a rugged individualist and self-made man.

to our enslavement without at least one noble effort to be free. We met often, and consulted frequently, and told our hopes and fears, recounted the difficulties, real and imagined, which we should be called on to meet. At times we were almost disposed to give up, and try to content ourselves with our wretched lot; at others, we were firm and unbending in our determination to go. Whenever we suggested any plan, there was shrinking—the odds were fearful. Our path was beset with the greatest obstacles; and if we succeeded in gaining the end of it, our right to be free was yet questionable—we were yet liable to be returned to bondage. We could see no spot, this side of the ocean, where we could be free. We knew nothing about Canada. Our knowledge of the north did not extend farther than New York; and to go there, and be forever harassed with the frightful liability of being returned to slavery—with the certainty of being treated tenfold worse than before—the thought was truly a horrible one, and one which it was not easy to overcome. The case sometimes stood thus: At every gate through which we were to pass, we saw a watchman—at every ferry a guard—on every bridge a sentinel—and in every wood a patrol. We were hemmed in upon every side. Here were the difficulties, real or imagined—the good to be sought, and the evil to be shunned. On the one hand, there stood slavery, a stern reality, glaring frightfully upon us,—its robes already crimsoned with the blood of millions, and even now feasting itself greedily upon our own flesh. On the other hand, away back in the dim distance, under the flickering light of the north star, behind some craggy hill or snow-covered mountain, stood a doubtful freedom—half frozen—beckoning us to come and share its hospitality. This in itself was sometimes enough to stagger us; but when we permitted ourselves to survey the road, we were frequently appalled. Upon either side we saw grim death, assuming the most horrid shapes. Now it was starvation, causing us to eat our own flesh;—now we were contending with the waves, and were drowned;—now we were overtaken, and torn to pieces by the fangs of the terrible bloodhound. We were stung by scorpions, chased by wild beasts, bitten by snakes, and finally, after having nearly reached the desired spot,—after swimming rivers, encountering wild beasts, sleeping in the woods, suffering hunger and nakedness,—we were overtaken by our pursuers, and, in our resistance, we were shot dead upon the spot! I say, this picture sometimes appalled us, and made us.

"rather bear those ills we had,
Than fly to others, that we knew not of."[86]

---

86. *Hamlet* 3:1. 81–82.

In coming to a fixed determination to run away, we did more than Patrick Henry,[87] when he resolved upon liberty or death. With us it was a doubtful liberty at most, and almost certain death if we failed. For my part, I should prefer death to hopeless bondage.

Sandy, one of our number, gave up the notion, but still encouraged us. Our company then consisted of Henry Harris, John Harris, Henry Bailey, Charles Roberts, and myself. Henry Bailey was my uncle, and belonged to my master. Charles married my aunt: he belonged to my master's father-in-law, Mr. William Hamilton.

The plan we finally concluded upon was, to get a large canoe belonging to Mr. Hamilton, and upon the Saturday night previous to Easter holidays, paddle directly up the Chesapeake Bay. On our arrival at the head of the bay, a distance of seventy or eighty miles from where we lived, it was our purpose to turn our canoe adrift, and follow the guidance of the north star till we got beyond the limits of Maryland. Our reason for taking the water route was, that we were less liable to be suspected as runaways; we hoped to be regarded as fishermen; whereas, if we should take the land route, we should be subjected to interruptions of almost every kind. Any one having a white face, and being so disposed, could stop us, and subject us to examination.

The week before our intended start, I wrote several protections, one for each of us. As well as I can remember, they were in the following words, to wit:—

"This is to certify that I, the undersigned, have given the bearer, my servant, full liberty to go to Baltimore, and spend the Easter holidays.
   Written with mine own hand, &c., 1835.
   "WILLIAM HAMILTON,
"Near St. Michael's, in Talbot county, Maryland."

We were not going to Baltimore; but, in going up the bay, we went toward Baltimore, and these protections were only intended to protect us while on the bay.

As the time drew near for our departure, our anxiety became more and more intense. It was truly a matter of life and death with us. The strength of

---

87. Douglass demonstrates here that he is not completely under the sway of Garrison, who cites Patrick Henry in his preface. Douglass points out that as a white slave owner, Patrick Henry did not face the same consequences during the American Revolution that Douglass and his fellow slaves did if they ran away. Early in their relationship, Douglass is already revealing a black perspective on American slavery that Garrison does not understand.

our determination was about to be fully tested. At this time, I was very active in explaining every difficulty, removing every doubt, dispelling every fear, and inspiring all with the firmness indispensable to success in our undertaking; assuring them that half was gained the instant we made the move; we had talked long enough; we were now ready to move; if not now, we never should be; and if we did not intend to move now, we had as well fold our arms, sit down, and acknowledge ourselves fit only to be slaves. This, none of us were prepared to acknowledge. Every man stood firm; and at our last meeting, we pledged ourselves afresh, in the most solemn manner, that, at the time appointed, we would certainly start in pursuit of freedom. This was in the middle of the week, at the end of which we were to be off. We went, as usual, to our several fields of labor, but with bosoms highly agitated with thoughts of our truly hazardous undertaking.[88] We tried to conceal our feelings as much as possible; and I think we succeeded very well.

After a painful waiting, the Saturday morning, whose night was to witness our departure, came. I hailed it with joy, bring what of sadness it might. Friday night was a sleepless one for me. I probably felt more anxious than the rest, because I was, by common consent, at the head of the whole affair. The responsibility of success or failure lay heavily upon me. The glory of the one, and the confusion of the other, were alike mine. The first two hours of that morning were such as I never experienced before, and hope never to again. Early in the morning, we went, as usual, to the field. We were spreading manure; and all at once, while thus engaged, I was overwhelmed with an indescribable feeling, in the fulness of which I turned to Sandy, who was near by, and said, "We are betrayed!" "Well," said he, "that thought has this moment struck me." We said no more. I was never more certain of any thing.

The horn was blown as usual, and we went up from the field to the house for breakfast. I went for the form, more than for want of any thing to eat that morning. Just as I got to the house, in looking out at the lane gate, I saw four white men, with two colored men. The white men were on horseback, and the colored ones were walking behind, as if tied. I watched them a few moments till they got up to our lane gate. Here they halted, and tied the colored men to the gate-post. I was not yet certain as to what the matter was. In a few moments, in rode Mr. Hamilton, with a speed betokening great excitement. He came to the door, and inquired if Master William was in. He was told he was at the barn. Mr. Hamilton, without dismounting, rode up to the barn with extraordinary speed. In a few

---

88. This genteel language, which sounds inflated and threadbare to modern readers, is what many nineteenth-century American readers regarded as appropriate diction and even a sign of refinement.

moments, he and Mr. Freeland returned to the house. By this time, the three constables rode up, and in great haste dismounted, tied their horses, and met Master William and Mr. Hamilton returning from the barn; and after talking awhile, they all walked up to the kitchen door. There was no one in the kitchen but myself and John. Henry and Sandy were up at the barn. Mr. Freeland put his head in at the door, and called me by name, saying, there were some gentlemen at the door who wished to see me. I stepped to the door, and inquired what they wanted. They at once seized me, and, without giving me any satisfaction, tied me—lashing my hands closely together. I insisted upon knowing what the matter was. They at length said, that they had learned I had been in a "scrape," and that I was to be examined before my master; and if their information proved false, I should not be hurt.

In a few moments, they succeeded in tying John. They then turned to Henry, who had by this time returned, and commanded him to cross his hands. "I won't!" said Henry, in a firm tone, indicating his readiness to meet the consequences of his refusal. "Won't you?" said Tom Graham, the constable. "No, I won't!" said Henry, in a still stronger tone. With this, two of the constables pulled out their shining pistols, and swore, by their Creator, that they would make him cross his hands or kill him. Each cocked his pistol, and, with fingers on the trigger, walked up to Henry, saying, at the same time, if he did not cross his hands, they would blow his damned heart out. "Shoot me, shoot me!" said Henry; "you can't kill me but once. Shoot, shoot,—and be damned! I won't be tied!" This he said in a tone of loud defiance; and at the same time, with a motion as quick as lightning, he with one single stroke dashed the pistols from the hand of each constable. As he did this, all hands fell upon him, and, after beating him some time, they finally overpowered him, and got him tied.

During the scuffle, I managed, I know not how, to get my pass out, and, without being discovered, put it into the fire. We were all now tied; and just as we were to leave for Easton jail, Betsy Freeland, mother of William Freeland, came to the door with her hands full of biscuits, and divided them between Henry and John. She then delivered herself of a speech, to the following effect:—addressing herself to me, she said, "You devil! You yellow devil! it was you that put it into the heads of Henry and John to run away. But for you, you long-legged mulatto devil! Henry nor John would never have thought of such a thing." I made no reply, and was immediately hurried off towards St. Michael's. Just a moment previous to the scuffle with Henry, Mr. Hamilton suggested the propriety of making a search for the protections which he had understood Frederick had written for himself and the rest. But, just at the moment he was about carrying his proposal into effect, his aid was needed in helping to tie Henry; and the excitement attending the scuffle caused them either to forget, or to deem it unsafe, under the circumstances, to search. So we were not yet convicted of the intention to run away.

When we got about half way to St. Michael's, while the constables having us in charge were looking ahead, Henry inquired of me what he should do with his pass. I told him to eat it with his biscuit, and own nothing; and we passed the word around, "*Own nothing*;" and "*Own nothing!*" said we all. Our confidence in each other was unshaken. We were resolved to succeed or fail together, after the calamity had befallen us as much as before. We were now prepared for any thing. We were to be dragged that morning fifteen miles behind horses, and then to be placed in the Easton jail. When we reached St. Michael's, we underwent a sort of examination. We all denied that we ever intended to run away. We did this more to bring out the evidence against us, than from any hope of getting clear of being sold; for, as I have said, we were ready for that. The fact was, we cared but little where we went, so we went together. Our greatest concern was about separation. We dreaded that more than any thing this side of death. We found the evidence against us to be the testimony of one person; our master would not tell who it was; but we came to a unanimous decision among ourselves as to who their informant was.[89] We were sent off to the jail at Easton. When we got there, we were delivered up to the sheriff, Mr. Joseph Graham, and by him placed in jail. Henry, John, and myself, were placed in one room together—Charles, and Henry Bailey, in another. Their object in separating us was to hinder concert.

We had been in jail scarcely twenty minutes, when a swarm of slave traders, and agents for slave traders, flocked into jail to look at us, and to ascertain if we were for sale. Such a set of beings I never saw before! I felt myself surrounded by so many fiends from perdition. A band of pirates never looked more like their father, the devil. They laughed and grinned over us, saying, "Ah, my boys! we have got you, haven't we?" And after taunting us in various ways, they one by one went into an examination of us, with intent to ascertain our value. They would impudently ask us if we would not like to have them for our masters. We would make them no answer, and leave them to find out as best they could. Then they would curse and swear at us, telling us that they could take the devil out of us in a very little while, if we were only in their hands.

While in jail, we found ourselves in much more comfortable quarters than we expected when we went there. We did not get much to eat, nor that which was very good; but we had a good clean room, from the windows of which we could see what was going on in the street, which was very much better than though we had been placed in one of the dark, damp cells.

---

89. In his third autobiography, *The Life and Times of Frederick Douglass* (1882), Douglass identifies the informant as Sandy Jenkins, the same man who told Douglass about carrying a root for protection against threats.

Upon the whole, we got along very well, so far as the jail and its keeper were concerned. Immediately after the holidays were over, contrary to all our expectations, Mr. Hamilton and Mr. Freeland came up to Easton, and took Charles, the two Henrys, and John, out of jail, and carried them home, leaving me alone. I regarded this separation as a final one. It caused me more pain than any thing else in the whole transaction. I was ready for any thing rather than separation. I supposed that they had consulted together, and had decided that, as I was the whole cause of the intention of the others to run away, it was hard to make the innocent suffer with the guilty; and that they had, therefore, concluded to take the others home, and sell me, as a warning to the others that remained. It is due to the noble Henry to say, he seemed almost as reluctant at leaving the prison as at leaving home to come to the prison. But we knew we should, in all probability, be separated, if we were sold; and since he was in their hands, he concluded to go peaceably home.

I was now left to my fate. I was all alone, and within the walls of a stone prison. But a few days before, and I was full of hope. I expected to have been safe in a land of freedom; but now I was covered with gloom, sunk down to the utmost despair. I thought the possibility of freedom was gone. I was kept in this way about one week, at the end of which, Captain Auld, my master, to my surprise and utter astonishment, came up, and took me out, with the intention of sending me, with a gentleman of his acquaintance, into Alabama. But, from some cause or other, he did not send me to Alabama, but concluded to send me back to Baltimore, to live again with his brother Hugh, and to learn a trade.

Thus, after an absence of three years and one month, I was once more permitted to return to my old home at Baltimore. My master sent me away, because there existed against me a very great prejudice in the community, and he feared I might be killed.

In a few weeks after I went to Baltimore, Master Hugh hired me to Mr. William Gardner, an extensive ship-builder, on Fell's Point. I was put there to learn how to calk.[90] It, however, proved a very unfavorable place for the accomplishment of this object. Mr. Gardner was engaged that spring in building two large man-of-war brigs, professedly for the Mexican government. The vessels were to be launched in the July of that year, and in failure thereof, Mr. Gardner was to lose a considerable sum; so that when I entered, all was hurry. There was no time to learn any thing. Every man had to do that which he knew how to do. In entering the shipyard, my

---

90. It is possible that some of the ships on which Douglass worked as a calker (he became quite capable at this use of tar to make a ship water-tight) became slave ships, a particularly sad irony. "Calk" is equivalent to our "caulk."

orders from Mr. Gardner were, to do whatever the carpenters commanded me to do. This was placing me at the beck and call of about seventy-five men. I was to regard all these as masters. Their word was to be my law. My situation was a most trying one. At times I needed a dozen pair of hands. I was called a dozen ways in the space of a single minute. Three or four voices would strike my ear at the same moment. It was—"Fred., come help me to cant this timber here."—"Fred., come carry this timber yonder."—"Fred., bring that roller here."—"Fred., go get a fresh can of water."—"Fred., come help saw off the end of this timber."—"Fred., go quick, and get the crowbar."—"Fred., hold on the end of this fall."—"Fred., go to the blacksmith's shop, and get a new punch."—"Hurra, Fred! run and bring me a cold chisel."[91]—"I say, Fred., bear a hand, and get up a fire as quick as lightning under that steam-box."—"Halloo, nigger! come, turn this grindstone."—"Come, come! move, move! and bowse this timber forward."—"I say, darky, blast your eyes, why don't you heat up some pitch?"—"Halloo! halloo! halloo!" (Three voices at the same time.) "Come here!—Go there!—Hold on where you are! Damn you, if you move, I'll knock your brains out!"

This was my school for eight months; and I might have remained there longer, but for a most horrid fight I had with four of the white apprentices, in which my left eye was nearly knocked out, and I was horribly mangled in other respects. The facts in the case were these: Until a very little while after I went there, white and black ship-carpenters worked side by side, and no one seemed to see any impropriety in it. All hands seemed to be very well satisfied. Many of the black carpenters were freemen. Things seemed to be going on very well. All at once, the white carpenters knocked off, and said they would not work with free colored workmen. Their reason for this, as alleged, was, that if free colored carpenters were encouraged, they would soon take the trade into their own hands, and poor white men would be thrown out of employment. They therefore felt called upon at once to put a stop to it. And, taking advantage of Mr. Gardner's necessities, they broke off, swearing they would work no longer, unless he would discharge his black carpenters. Now, though this did not extend to me in form, it did reach me in fact. My fellow-apprentices very soon began to feel it degrading to them to work with me. They began to put on airs, and talk about the "niggers" taking the country, saying we all ought to be killed; and, being encouraged by the journeymen, they commenced making my condition as hard as they could, by hectoring me around, and sometimes striking me. I, of course, kept the vow I made after the fight with Mr. Covey, and struck back again, regardless of consequences; and

---

91. A chisel used for cutting metal.

while I kept them from combining, I succeeded very well; for I could whip the whole of them, taking them separately. They, however, at length combined, and came upon me, armed with sticks, stones, and heavy handspikes. One came in front with a half brick. There was one at each side of me, and one behind me. While I was attending to those in front, and on either side, the one behind ran up with the handspike, and struck me a heavy blow upon the head. It stunned me. I fell, and with this they all ran upon me, and fell to beating me with their fists. I let them lay on for a while, gathering strength. In an instant, I gave a sudden surge, and rose to my hands and knees. Just as I did that, one of their number gave me, with his heavy boot, a powerful kick in the left eye. My eyeball seemed to have burst. When they saw my eye closed, and badly swollen, they left me. With this I seized the handspike, and for a time pursued them. But here the carpenters interfered, and I thought I might as well give it up. It was impossible to stand my hand against so many. All this took place in sight of not less than fifty white ship-carpenters, and not one interposed a friendly word; but some cried, "Kill the damned nigger! Kill him! kill him! He struck a white person." I found my only chance for life was in flight. I succeeded in getting away without an additional blow, and barely so; for to strike a white man is death by Lynch[92] law,—and that was the law in Mr. Gardner's ship-yard; nor is there much of any other out of Mr. Gardner's ship-yard.

I went directly home, and told the story of my wrongs to Master Hugh; and I am happy to say of him, irreligious as he was, his conduct

---

92. Lynching is one of the darkest episodes in American history. Legislation against it at the federal level did not pass until well into the twentieth century. The groups most likely to be lynched were black males, then white males, then black women, then white women. It was not restricted to hanging victims with a rope, but also included driving long nails into a barrel, and rolling it down a hill, as Ida B. Wells reports in *A Red Record* (1895). Many lynchings were documented by white newspapers printing accounts of them. Picture post-cards with pictures of these atrocities were sent through the United States postal service, and in some instances extra train cars were added for the crowds that wanted to watch; cigarette butts, peanut shells, and whisky bottles were left at the sights, as if there had been a picnic. For an extremely powerful indictment of the grisly process of lynching, many readers have gone to James Baldwin's short story, "Going to Meet the Man." There were no trials; the problem grew worse after the Civil War, partly because some whites in the South wanted to blame black people for the South's defeat. The usual rationale was the rape of a white woman, but the question that could have been asked was why, when white veterans had returned to the South after 1865, could the rape of white women by black men have surged, and been far less before the war ended, when many whites from the South were off fighting? Readers who want to know more about this grim spectacle should consult James Allen, *Without Sanctuary: Lynching Photography in America* (Santa Fe, NM, 2000); it contains documentation of lynchings in print and in photographic images.

was heavenly, compared with that of his brother Thomas under similar circumstances. He listened attentively to my narration of the circumstances leading to the savage outrage, and gave many proofs of his strong indignation at it. The heart of my once overkind mistress was again melted into pity. My puffed-out eye and blood-covered face moved her to tears. She took a chair by me, washed the blood from my face, and, with a mother's tenderness, bound up my head, covering the wounded eye with a lean piece of fresh beef. It was almost compensation for my suffering to witness, once more, a manifestation of kindness from this, my once affectionate old mistress. Master Hugh was very much enraged. He gave expression to his feelings by pouring out curses upon the heads of those who did the deed. As soon as I got a little the better of my bruises, he took me with him to Esquire Watson's, on Bond Street, to see what could be done about the matter. Mr. Watson inquired who saw the assault committed. Master Hugh told him it was done in Mr. Gardner's ship-yard at midday, where there were a large company of men at work. "As to that," he said, "the deed was done, and there was no question as to who did it." His answer was, he could do nothing in the case, unless some white man would come forward and testify. He could issue no warrant on my word. If I had been killed in the presence of a thousand colored people, their testimony combined would have been insufficient to have arrested one of the murderers. Master Hugh, for once, was compelled to say this state of things was too bad. Of course, it was impossible to get any white man to volunteer his testimony in my behalf, and against the white young men. Even those who may have sympathized with me were not prepared to do this. It required a degree of courage unknown to them to do so; for just at that time, the slightest manifestation of humanity toward a colored person was denounced as abolitionism, and that name subjected its bearer to frightful liabilities. The watchwords of the bloody-minded in that region, and in those days, were, "Damn the abolitionists!" and "Damn the niggers!" There was nothing done, and probably nothing would have been done if I had been killed. Such was, and such remains, the state of things in the Christian city of Baltimore.

Master Hugh, finding he could get no redress, refused to let me go back again to Mr. Gardner. He kept me himself, and his wife dressed my wound till I was again restored to health. He then took me into the ship-yard of which he was foreman, in the employment of Mr. Walter Price. There I was immediately set to calking, and very soon learned the art of using my mallet and irons. In the course of one year from the time I left Mr. Gardner's, I was able to command the highest wages given to the most experienced calkers. I was now of some importance to my master. I was bringing him from six to seven dollars per week. I sometimes brought him nine dollars per week: my wages were a dollar and a half a day. After learning how to calk, I sought my own employment, made my own contracts, and collected the money which I earned. My pathway became much more smooth than before; my condition was now much more comfortable. When I could get no calking to do, I did nothing. During these leisure times, those old notions about freedom would steal over me again. When in Mr. Gardner's employment, I was kept in such a perpetual whirl of excitement, I could think of nothing, scarcely, but my life; and in thinking of my life, I almost forgot my liberty. I have observed this in my experience of slavery,—that whenever my condition was improved, instead of its increasing my contentment, it only increased my desire to be free, and set me to thinking of plans to gain my freedom. I have found that, to make a contented slave, it is necessary to make a thoughtless one. It is necessary to darken his moral and mental vision, and, as far as possible, to annihilate the power of reason. He must be able to detect no inconsistencies in slavery; he must be made to feel that slavery is right; and he can be brought to that only when he ceases to be a man.

I was now getting, as I have said, one dollar and fifty cents per day. I contracted for it; I earned it; it was paid to me; it was rightfully my own; yet, upon each returning Saturday night, I was compelled to deliver every cent of that money to Master Hugh. And why? Not because he earned it,—not because he had any hand in earning it,—not because I owed it to him,—nor because he possessed the slightest shadow of a right to it; but solely because he had the power to compel me to give it up. The right of the grim-visaged pirate upon the high seas is exactly the same.[93]

CHAPTER XI

I now come to that part of my life during which I planned, and finally succeeded in making, my escape from slavery. But before narrating any of the peculiar circumstances, I deem it proper to make known my intention not to state all the facts connected with the transaction. My reasons for pursuing this course may be understood from the following: First, were I to give a minute statement of all the facts, it is not only possible, but quite probable, that others would thereby be involved in the most embarrassing difficulties. Secondly, such a statement would most undoubtedly induce greater vigilance on the part of slaveholders than has existed heretofore among them; which would, of course, be the means of guarding a door whereby some dear brother bondman might escape his galling chains. I

---

93. Douglass omits from this chapter that Captain Thomas Auld told him he would free him on his twenty-fifth birthday, which some readers believe puts the captain in a better light; others feel that he should have freed him sooner.

deeply regret the necessity that impels me to suppress any thing of importance connected with my experience in slavery. It would afford me great pleasure indeed, as well as materially add to the interest of my narrative, were I at liberty to gratify a curiosity, which I know exists in the minds of many, by an accurate statement of all the facts pertaining to my most fortunate escape. But I must deprive myself of this pleasure, and the curious of the gratification which such a statement would afford. I would allow myself to suffer under the greatest imputations which evil-minded men might suggest, rather than exculpate myself, and thereby run the hazard of closing the slightest avenue by which a brother slave might clear himself of the chains and fetters of slavery.

I have never approved of the very public manner in which some of our western friends have conducted what they call the underground railroad,[94] but which I think, by their open declarations, has been made most emphatically the upper-ground railroad. I honor those good men and women for their noble daring, and applaud them for willingly subjecting themselves to bloody persecution, by openly avowing their participation in the escape of slaves. I, however, can see very little good resulting from such a course, either to themselves or the slaves escaping; while, upon the other hand, I see and feel assured that those open declarations are a positive evil to the slaves remaining, who are seeking to escape. They do nothing towards enlightening the slave, whilst they do much towards enlightening the master. They stimulate him to greater watchfulness, and enhance his power to capture his slave. We owe something to the slave south of the line[95] as well as to those north of it; and in aiding the latter on their way to freedom, we should be careful to do nothing which would be likely to

---

94. Neither underground nor a railroad, the "Underground Railroad" was actually a series of safe houses from the South to the North that provided black "passengers" a means of escaping slavery. Often sick, hungry, cold, and terrified, thousands of African American slaves escaped to the North and Canada by means of this secret arrangement, managed by blacks and whites. The Quakers were particularly noteworthy for participating in the Underground Railroad; they helped with food, clothing, medicine, money, and moral support. Harriet Tubman was an outstanding "black engineer" on this network, helping numerous slaves escape. It should be noted also that "many fugitive slaves successfully escaped to free black communities in the South, . . . in larger cities such as Louisville, Kentucky, and New Orleans. Over in those communities, some escaped slaves managed to conceal themselves with relative ease. Not surprisingly, many slave-state legislatures passed laws to restrict the liberties of free blacks or even banish them from their states. Efforts to banish free blacks had little success, however. In the three decades before the Civil War, the free black population increased in at least ten of the largest cities in slave states" (quoted from Richard C. Wade, *Slavery in the Cities*, Oxford University Press, 1964, 325–327, by Ranjit S. Dighe, ed., *The Historian's "Huck Finn,"* Praeger, 2016, 126 fn. 71).

95. The Mason-Dixon line.

hinder the former from escaping from slavery. I would keep the merciless slaveholder profoundly ignorant of the means of flight adopted by the slave. I would leave him to imagine himself surrounded by myriads of invisible tormentors, ever ready to snatch from his infernal grasp his trembling prey. Let him be left to feel his way in the dark; let darkness commensurate with his crime hover over him; and let him feel that at every step he takes, in pursuit of the flying bondman, he is running the frightful risk of having his hot brains dashed out by an invisible agency. Let us render the tyrant no aid; let us not hold the light by which he can trace the footprints of our flying brother. But enough of this. I will now proceed to the statement of those facts, connected with my escape, for which I am alone responsible, and for which no one can be made to suffer but myself.

In the early part of the year 1838, I became quite restless. I could see no reason why I should, at the end of each week, pour the reward of my toil into the purse of my master. When I carried to him my weekly wages, he would, after counting the money, look me in the face with a robber-like fierceness, and ask, "Is this all?" He was satisfied with nothing less than the last cent. He would, however, when I made him six dollars, sometimes give me six cents, to encourage me. It had the opposite effect. I regarded it as a sort of admission of my right to the whole. The fact that he gave me any part of my wages was proof, to my mind, that he believed me entitled to the whole of them. I always felt worse for having received any thing; for I feared that the giving me a few cents would ease his conscience, and make him feel himself to be a pretty honorable sort of robber. My discontent grew upon me. I was ever on the look-out for means of escape; and, finding no direct means, I determined to try to hire my time, with a view of getting money with which to make my escape. In the spring of 1838, when Master Thomas came to Baltimore to purchase his spring goods, I got an opportunity, and applied to him to allow me to hire my time. He unhesitatingly refused my request, and told me this was another stratagem by which to escape. He told me I could go nowhere but that he could get me; and that, in the event of my running away, he should spare no pains in his efforts to catch me. He exhorted me to content myself, and be obedient. He told me, if I would be happy, I must lay out no plans for the future. He said, if I behaved myself properly, he would take care of me. Indeed, he advised me to complete thoughtlessness of the future, and taught me to depend solely upon him for happiness. He seemed to see fully the pressing necessity of setting aside my intellectual nature, in order to contentment in slavery. But in spite of him, and even in spite of myself, I continued to think, and to think about the injustice of my enslavement, and the means of escape.

About two months after this, I applied to Master Hugh for the privilege of hiring my time. He was not acquainted with the fact that I had applied to Master Thomas, and had been refused. He too, at first, seemed disposed to refuse; but, after some reflection, he granted me the privilege, and proposed the following terms: I was to be allowed all my time, make all contracts with those for whom I worked, and find my own employment; and, in return for this liberty, I was to pay him three dollars at the end of each week; find myself in calking tools,[96] and in board and clothing. My board was two dollars and a half per week. This, with the wear and tear of clothing and calking tools, made my regular expenses about six dollars per week. This amount I was compelled to make up, or relinquish the privilege of hiring my time. Rain or shine, work or no work, at the end of each week the money must be forthcoming, or I must give up my privilege. This arrangement, it will be perceived, was decidedly in my master's favor. It relieved him of all need of looking after me. His money was sure. He received all the benefits of slaveholding without its evils; while I endured all the evils of a slave, and suffered all the care and anxiety of a freeman. I found it a hard bargain. But, hard as it was, I thought it better than the old mode of getting along. It was a step towards freedom to be allowed to bear the responsibilities of a freeman, and I was determined to hold on upon it.

---

96. The reference to calking initiates a continued series of provocative details that suggests Herman Melville in *Benito Cereno* may have been thinking of Frederick Douglass, perhaps as Atufal, Babo's right-hand man in the slave revolt on board the slave ship *San Dominick*. Melville is known for using his fiction as political and social allegories, so it is not surprising that Atufal is an Ashanti and Douglass was partly descended from that African people. Douglass was a tall, physically imposing man, as was Atufal. Douglass also had a considerable background in building ships, as he hired himself out to a shipbuilder in the 1845 *Narrative* as a calker (a laborer who seals the seams between the boards that wooden ships were made of in the nineteenth century). *Benito Cereno* is very much about the two ships *San Dominick* and *Bachelor's Delight*. Moreover, in the 1845 *Narrative* Douglass speaks of seizing a handspike when he is defending himself against some white laborers at the shipyard; handspikes are used by the Africans against the American sailors, although Atufal and other Ashanti fought with hatchets. In addition, Douglass published *The Heroic Slave* in 1853, two years before *Benito Cereno* was published; in it, the hero, Madison Washington, leads a successful slave revolt on the *Creole*; violence served a noble purpose, because Washington and his fellow Africans eventually gain their freedom. But the violence on board *San Dominick* leads to the death of Atufal and the defeat of the other Africans. Much of the violence on *San Dominick* is a result of Babo's murderous hatred of the Spanish crew (the owner of the slaves, Alexandro Aranda, ends up as a skeleton on the prow of *San Dominick*). Melville sometimes entertained notions of an African like Atufal as a Noble Savage, but Atufal, although he killed no one, was a leader of the insurrection against the Spanish. If Melville did indeed have Douglass in mind when he wrote *Benito Cereno*, he may have been issuing a warning to his readers in 1855 of a black insurrection against American slavery, particularly if led by men like Atufal, who was wrapped in chains, to fool the American captain Amasa Delano in *Benito Cereno*, chains that could quickly be removed if need be.

I bent myself to the work of making money. I was ready to work at night as well as day, and by the most untiring perseverance and industry, I made enough to meet my expenses, and lay up a little money every week. I went on thus from May till August. Master Hugh then refused to allow me to hire my time longer. The ground for his refusal was a failure on my part, one Saturday night, to pay him for my week's time. This failure was occasioned by my attending a camp meeting about ten miles from Baltimore. During the week, I had entered into an engagement with a number of young friends to start from Baltimore to the camp ground early Saturday evening; and being detained by my employer, I was unable to get down to Master Hugh's without disappointing the company. I knew that Master Hugh was in no special need of the money that night. I therefore decided to go to camp meeting, and upon my return pay him the three dollars. I staid at the camp meeting one day longer than I intended when I left. But as soon as I returned, I called upon him to pay him what he considered his due. I found him very angry; he could scarce restrain his wrath. He said he had a great mind to give me a severe whipping. He wished to know how I dared go out of the city without asking his permission. I told him I hired my time and while I paid him the price which he asked for it, I did not know that I was bound to ask him when and where I should go. This reply troubled him; and, after reflecting a few moments, he turned to me, and said I should hire my time no longer; that the next thing he should know of, I would be running away. Upon the same plea, he told me to bring my tools and clothing home forthwith. I did so; but instead of seeking work, as I had been accustomed to do previously to hiring my time, I spent the whole week without the performance of a single stroke of work. I did this in retaliation. Saturday night, he called upon me as usual for my week's wages. I told him I had no wages; I had done no work that week. Here we were upon the point of coming to blows. He raved, and swore his determination to get hold of me. I did not allow myself a single word; but was resolved, if he laid the weight of his hand upon me, it should be blow for blow. He did not strike me, but told me that he would find me in constant employment in future. I thought the matter over during the next day, Sunday, and finally resolved upon the third day of September, as the day upon which I would make a second attempt to secure my freedom. I now had three weeks during which to prepare for my journey. Early on Monday morning, before Master Hugh had time to make any engagement for me, I went out and got employment of Mr. Butler, at his ship-yard near the drawbridge, upon what is called the City Block, thus making it unnecessary for him to seek employment for me. At the end of the week, I brought him between eight and nine dollars. He seemed very well pleased, and asked why I did not do the same the week before. He little knew what my plans were. My object in working steadily was to remove any suspicion he might entertain of my intent to run away; and in this I succeeded admirably. I suppose he thought I was never better satisfied with my condition than at the very time during which I was planning my escape. The second week passed, and again I carried him my full wages; and so well pleased was he, that he gave me twenty-five cents, (quite a large sum for a slaveholder to give a slave,) and bade me to make a good use of it. I told him I would.[97]

Things went on without very smoothly indeed, but within there was trouble.[98] It is impossible for me to describe my feelings as the time of my contemplated start drew near. I had a number of warmhearted friends[99] in Baltimore,—friends that I loved almost as I did my life,—and the thought of being separated from them forever was painful beyond expression. It is my opinion that thousands would escape from slavery, who now remain, but for the strong cords of affection that bind them to their friends. The thought of leaving my friends was decidedly the most painful thought with which I had to contend. The love of them was my tender point, and shook my decision more than all things else. Besides the pain of separation, the

---

97. This is just one of several instances of Douglass's emphasis on black capitalism as a means to black self-sufficiency and as a means to increasing black options. In this and other ways, he is in the same tradition Benjamin Franklin heads—in America money is a key means of getting ahead.

98. Contrast Madison Washington's escape from slavery with Douglass's: eight years after he published his 1845 *Narrative*, Douglass published his only work of prose fiction, *The Heroic Slave* (1853). In it, the slave of the title, Madison Washington, like Douglass, also escaped from bondage, but Washington, who is based on the historical Madison Washington who led a successful slave mutiny on board the slave ship *Creole* in 1841, openly acknowledges and celebrates his wife and her crucial support in his efforts to escape:

"I will try to tell you," said Madison. "Just four weeks after that Sabbath morning, I gathered up the few rags of clothing I had, and started, as I supposed, for the North and for freedom. I must not stop to describe my feelings on taking this step. It seemed like taking a leap into the dark. The thought of leaving my poor wife and two little children caused me indescribable anguish; but consoling myself with the reflection that once free, I could, possibly, devise ways and means to gain their freedom also, I nerved myself up to make the attempt. I started, but ill-luck attended me; for after being out a whole week, strange to say, I still found myself on my master's grounds; the third night after being out, a season of clouds and rain set in, wholly preventing me from seeing the North Star, which I had trusted as my guide, not dreaming that clouds might intervene between us." (*The Heroic Slave*, p. 189, in *Autographs for Freedom*, ed. Julia Griffiths, Boston, 1853).

Was Douglass trying to compensate for his superficial treatment of his own wife's support in his escape from slavery? Washington also refers to his wife Susan Washington as his "good angel," a term Douglass never comes close to in his treatment of Anne Murray Douglass in his 1845 *Narrative*.

99. Friendship was of paramount value to Douglass. He always had a deep need for it and an intense affection for his friends. They ranged from Lincoln to Gerrit Smith, John Brown, Julia Griffiths, William Lloyd Garrison, Ottilie Assing, James McCune Smith, Ida B. Wells, and many others, some of whom remain anonymous. He relied on his friends for emotional, social, and sometimes financial support.

dread and apprehension of a failure exceeded what I had experienced at my first attempt. The appalling defeat I then sustained returned to torment me. I felt assured that, if I failed in this attempt, my case would be a hopeless one—it would seal my fate as a slave forever. I could not hope to get off with any thing less than the severest punishment, and being placed beyond the means of escape. It required no very vivid imagination to depict the most frightful scenes through which I should have to pass, in case I failed. The wretchedness of slavery, and the blessedness of freedom, were perpetually before me. It was life and death with me. But I remained firm, and, according to my resolution, on the third day of September, 1838, I left my chains, and succeeded in reaching New York without the slightest interruption of any kind. How I did so,—what means I adopted,—what direction I travelled, and by what mode of conveyance,—I must leave unexplained, for the reasons before mentioned.[100]

I have been frequently asked how I felt when I found myself in a free State. I have never been able to answer the question with any satisfaction to myself. It was a moment of the highest excitement I ever experienced. I suppose I felt as one may imagine the unarmed mariner to feel when he is rescued by a friendly man-of-war from the pursuit of a pirate. In writing to a dear friend, immediately after my arrival at New York, I said I felt like one who had escaped a den of hungry lions. This state of mind, however, very soon subsided; and I was again seized with a feeling of great insecurity and loneliness. I was yet liable to be taken back, and subjected to all the tortures of slavery. This in itself was enough to damp the ardor of my enthusiasm. But the loneliness overcame me. There I was in the midst of thousands, and yet a perfect stranger; without home and without friends, in the midst of thousands of my own brethren—children of a common Father, and yet I dared not to unfold to any one of them my sad condition. I was afraid to speak to any one for fear of speaking to the wrong one, and thereby falling into the hands of money-loving kidnappers, whose business it was to lie in wait for the panting fugitive, as the ferocious beasts of the forest lie in wait for their prey. The motto which I adopted when I started from slavery was this—"Trust no man!" I saw in every white man an enemy, and in almost every colored man cause for distrust. It was a most painful situation; and, to understand it, one must needs experience it, or imagine himself in similar circumstances. Let him be a fugitive slave in a strange land—a land given up to be the hunting-ground for slaveholders—whose inhabitants are legalized kidnappers—where he is every moment subjected to the terrible liability of being seized upon by his

---

100. In later versions of his life's history, Douglass was more candid about these details, because the people he names are dead, and supposedly African Americans can leave the South without hindrance after 1865.

fellowmen, as the hideous crocodile seizes upon his prey!—I say, let him place himself in my situation—without home or friends—without money or credit—wanting shelter, and no one to give it—wanting bread, and no money to buy it,—and at the same time let him feel that he is pursued by merciless men-hunters, and in total darkness as to what to do, where to go, or where to stay,—perfectly helpless both as to the means of defence and means of escape,—in the midst of plenty, yet suffering the terrible gnawings of hunger,—in the midst of houses, yet having no home,—among fellow-men, yet feeling as if in the midst of wild beasts, whose greediness to swallow up the trembling and half-famished fugitive is only equalled by that with which the monsters of the deep swallow up the helpless fish upon which they subsist,—I say, let him be placed in this most trying situation,—the situation in which I was placed,—then, and not till then, will he fully appreciate the hardships of, and know how to sympathize with, the toil-worn and whip-scarred fugitive slave.

Thank Heaven, I remained but a short time in this distressed situation. I was relieved from it by the humane hand of *Mr. David Ruggles*,[101] whose vigilance, kindness, and perseverance, I shall never forget. I am glad of an opportunity to express, as far as words can, the love and gratitude I bear him. Mr. Ruggles is now afflicted with blindness, and is himself in need of the same kind offices which he was once so forward in the performance of toward others. I had been in New York but a few days, when Mr. Ruggles sought me out, and very kindly took me to his boarding-house at the corner of Church and Lespenard Streets. Mr. Ruggles was then very deeply engaged in the memorable *Darg* case,[102] as well as attending to a number of other fugitive slaves, devising ways and means for their successful escape; and, though watched and hemmed in on almost every side, he seemed to be more than a match for his enemies.

Very soon after I went to Mr. Ruggles, he wished to know of me where I wanted to go; as he deemed it unsafe for me to remain in New York. I told him I was a calker, and should like to go where I could get work. I thought of going to Canada; but he decided against it, and in favor of my going to New Bedford, thinking I should be able to get work there at my trade. At this time, Anna,*[103] my intended wife, came on; for I wrote to her immediately after my arrival at New York, (notwithstanding my homeless,

---

101. Ruggles (1810–1849) was an important black abolitionist who helped Douglass in his self-emancipation.

102. Ruggles had been helping a fugitive slave owned by a white man named John Darg, who also accused the fugitive of stealing from him.

103. She was Douglass's first wife. A free black woman, she also helped Douglass escape, but unfortunately, she was barely literate and not very much is known about her. Douglass is not forthcoming about her.

houseless, and helpless condition,) informing her of my successful flight, and wishing her to come on forthwith. In a few days after her arrival, Mr. Ruggles called in the Rev. J. W. C. Pennington,[104] who, in the presence of Mr. Ruggles, Mrs. Michaels, and two or three others, performed the marriage ceremony, and gave us a certificate, of which the following is an exact copy:—

> "This may certify, that I joined together in holy matrimony Frederick Johnson** and Anna Murray, as man and wife, in the presence of Mr. David Ruggles and Mrs. Michaels.
>
> "JAMES W. C. PENNINGTON
> "New York, Sept. 15, 1838"
> *She was free.
> **I had changed my name from Frederick Bailey to that of Johnson.

Upon receiving this certificate, and a five-dollar bill from Mr. Ruggles, I shouldered one part of our baggage, and Anna took up the other, and we set out forthwith to take passage on board of the steamboat John W. Richmond for Newport, on our way to New Bedford. Mr. Ruggles gave me a letter to a Mr. Shaw in Newport, and told me, in case my money did not serve me to New Bedford, to stop in Newport and obtain further assistance; but upon our arrival at Newport, we were so anxious to get to a place of safety, that, notwithstanding we lacked the necessary money to pay our fare, we decided to take seats in the stage, and promise to pay when we got to New Bedford. We were encouraged to do this by two excellent gentlemen, residents of New Bedford, whose names I afterward ascertained to be Joseph Ricketson and William C. Taber.[105] They seemed at once to understand our circumstances, and gave us such assurance of their friendliness as put us fully at ease in their presence.

It was good indeed to meet with such friends, at such a time. Upon reaching New Bedford, we were directed to the house of Mr. Nathan

---

104. Another important black abolitionist; he was also a preacher. That white authors did not feel the need to reproduce a marriage certificate indicates how important Douglass thought it was to reproduce his. Because slave marriages before the end of the Civil War were not legal, Douglass wants it known that his to Anna Murray was legal. Even when slave marriages began to be acknowledged as legal, word did not reach all the remote parts of the South for years. Charles Chesnutt presents an interesting result of this problem in "The Wife of His Youth," a short story about a black woman who spent twenty-five years looking for her lost husband; she finds him as he is about to marry a much younger, light-skinned black woman who is a member of the Blue Vein Society, the membership of which is restricted to black people whose veins can be seen through their skin.

105. Prominent citizens of New Bedford.

Johnson, by whom we were kindly received, and hospitably provided for. Both Mr. and Mrs. Johnson[106] took a deep and lively interest in our welfare. They proved themselves quite worthy of the name of abolitionists. When the stage-driver found us unable to pay our fare, he held on upon our baggage as security for the debt. I had but to mention the fact to Mr. Johnson, and he forthwith advanced the money.

We now began to feel a degree of safety, and to prepare ourselves for the duties and responsibilities of a life of freedom. On the morning after our arrival at New Bedford, while at the breakfast-table, the question arose as to what name I should be called by. The name given me by my mother was, "Frederick Augustus Washington Bailey." I, however, had dispensed with the two middle names long before I left Maryland so that I was generally known by the name of "Frederick Bailey." I started from Baltimore bearing the name of "Stanley." When I got to New York, I again changed my name to "Frederick Johnson," and thought that would be the last change. But when I got to New Bedford, I found it necessary again to change my name. The reason of this necessity was, that there were so many Johnsons in New Bedford, it was already quite difficult to distinguish between them. I gave Mr. Johnson the privilege of choosing me a name, but told him he must not take from me the name of "Frederick." I must hold on to that, to preserve a sense of my identity. Mr. Johnson had just been reading the "Lady of the Lake," and at once suggested that my name be "Douglass." From that time until now I have been called "Frederick Douglass;" and as I am more widely known by that name than by either of the others, I shall continue to use it as my own.[107]

I was quite disappointed at the general appearance of things in New Bedford. The impression which I had received respecting the character and condition of the people of the north, I found to be singularly erroneous. I had very strangely supposed, while in slavery, that few of the comforts, and scarcely any of the luxuries, of life were enjoyed at the north, compared with what were enjoyed by the slaveholders of the south. I probably came to this conclusion from the fact that northern people owned no slaves. I supposed that they were about upon a level with the non-slaveholding

---

106. Prominent black abolitionists in New Bedford.

107. Douglass in Sir Walter Scott's poem, *The Lady of the Lake* (1810), is a heroic figure, like Frederick Douglass. Naming in African American experience has a particular resonance because so many enslaved black people were given only a single name, such as Cicero, a famous Roman orator; this verbal gesture was considered hilarious by whites because of the assumed absurdity of naming a slave after a famous white person. When they were given last names, such names were often those of their white owners, who might in fact be their fathers. Douglass is making a political statement here, because he is defining part of his identity; no black persons want to be called out of their name.

population of the south. I knew they were exceedingly poor, and I had been accustomed to regard their poverty as the necessary consequence of their being non-slaveholders. I had somehow imbibed the opinion that, in the absence of slaves, there could be no wealth, and very little refinement. And upon coming to the north, I expected to meet with a rough, hard-handed, and uncultivated population, living in the most Spartan-like[108] simplicity, knowing nothing of the ease, luxury, pomp, and grandeur of southern slaveholders. Such being my conjectures, any one acquainted with the appearance of New Bedford may very readily infer how palpably I must have seen my mistake.

In the afternoon of the day when I reached New Bedford, I visited the wharves, to take a view of the shipping. Here I found myself surrounded with the strongest proofs of wealth. Lying at the wharves, and riding in the stream, I saw many ships of the finest model, in the best order, and of the largest size. Upon the right and left, I was walled in by granite warehouses of the widest dimensions, stowed to their utmost capacity with the necessaries and comforts of life. Added to this, almost every body seemed to be at work, but noiselessly so, compared with what I had been accustomed to in Baltimore. There were no loud songs heard from those engaged in loading and unloading ships. I heard no deep oaths or horrid curses on the laborer. I saw no whipping of men; but all seemed to go smoothly on. Every man appeared to understand his work, and went at it with a sober, yet cheerful earnestness, which betokened the deep interest which he felt in what he was doing, as well as a sense of his own dignity as a man. To me this looked exceedingly strange. From the wharves I strolled around and over the town, gazing with wonder and admiration at the splendid churches, beautiful dwellings, and finely-cultivated gardens; evincing an amount of wealth, comfort, taste, and refinement, such as I had never seen in any part of slaveholding Maryland.

Every thing looked clean, new, and beautiful. I saw few or no dilapidated houses, with poverty-stricken inmates; no half-naked children and barefooted women, such as I had been accustomed to see in Hillsborough, Easton, St. Michael's, and Baltimore. The people looked more able, stronger, healthier, and happier, than those of Maryland. I was for once made glad by a view of extreme wealth, without being saddened by seeing extreme poverty. But the most astonishing as well as the most interesting thing to me was the condition of the colored people, a great many of whom, like myself, had escaped thither as a refuge from the hunters of men. I found many, who had not been seven years out of their chains, living in

---

108. The Spartans of ancient Greece are remembered for their extreme toughness and endurance.

finer houses, and evidently enjoying more of the comforts of life, than the average of slaveholders in Maryland. I will venture to assert, that my friend Mr. Nathan Johnson (of whom I can say with a grateful heart, "I was hungry, and he gave me meat; I was thirsty, and he gave me drink; I was a stranger, and he took me in") lived in a neater house; dined at a better table; took, paid for, and read, more newspapers; better understood the moral, religious, and political character of the nation,—than nine tenths of the slaveholders in Talbot county Maryland.[109] Yet Mr. Johnson was a working man. His hands were hardened by toil, and not his alone, but those also of Mrs. Johnson. I found the colored people much more spirited than I had supposed they would be. I found among them a determination to protect each other from the blood-thirsty kidnapper, at all hazards. Soon after my arrival, I was told of a circumstance which illustrated their spirit. A colored man and a fugitive slave were on unfriendly terms. The former was heard to threaten the latter with informing his master of his whereabouts. Straightway a meeting was called among the colored people, under the stereotyped notice, "Business of importance!" The betrayer was invited to attend. The people came at the appointed hour, and organized the meeting by appointing a very religious old gentleman as president, who, I believe, made a prayer, after which he addressed the meeting as follows: "*Friends, we have got him here, and I would recommend that you young men just take him outside the door, and kill him!*" With this, a number of them bolted at him; but they were intercepted by some more timid than themselves, and the betrayer escaped their vengeance, and has not been seen in New Bedford since. I believe there have been no more such threats, and should there be hereafter, I doubt not that death would be the consequence.

I found employment, the third day after my arrival, in stowing a sloop with a load of oil. It was new, dirty, and hard work for me; but I went at it with a glad heart and a willing hand. I was now my own master. It was a happy moment, the rapture of which can be understood only by those who have been slaves. It was the first work, the reward of which was to be entirely my own. There was no Master Hugh standing ready, the moment I earned the money, to rob me of it. I worked that day with a pleasure I had never before experienced. I was at work for myself and newly-married wife. It was to me the starting-point of a new existence. When I got through with that job, I went in pursuit of a job of calking; but such was the strength

---

109. Douglass may be seeing New Bedford through rose-colored glasses here, which, if true, would be understandable, as he does not yet fully know he, in some ways, has gone Up South, rather than Up North, that is, he will still be dealing with white racism even as a fugitive slave in the North. He will be much more candid about the North and its white abolitionists in *My Bondage and My Freedom* (1855).

of prejudice against color, among the white calkers, that they refused to work with me, and of course I could get no employment.*

* I am told that colored persons can now get employment at calking in New Bedford—a result of anti-slavery effort.

Finding my trade of no immediate benefit, I threw off my calking habiliments, and prepared myself to do any kind of work I could get to do. Mr. Johnson kindly let me have his wood-horse and saw, and I very soon found myself a plenty of work. There was no work too hard—none too dirty. I was ready to saw wood, shovel coal, carry wood, sweep the chimney, or roll oil casks,—all of which I did for nearly three years in New Bedford, before I became known to the anti-slavery world.

In about four months after I went to New Bedford, there came a young man to me, and inquired if I did not wish to take the "Liberator."[110] I told him I did; but, just having made my escape from slavery, I remarked that I was unable to pay for it then. I, however, finally became a subscriber to it. The paper came, and I read it from week to week with such feelings as it would be quite idle for me to attempt to describe. The paper became my meat and my drink. My soul was set all on fire. Its sympathy for my brethren in bonds—its scathing denunciations of slaveholders—its faithful exposures of slavery—and its powerful attacks upon the upholders of the institution—sent a thrill of joy through my soul, such as I had never felt before!

I had not long been a reader of the "Liberator," before I got a pretty correct idea of the principles, measures and spirit of the anti-slavery reform. I took right hold of the cause. I could do but little; but what I could, I did with a joyful heart, and never felt happier than when in an anti-slavery meeting. I seldom had much to say at the meetings, because what I wanted to say was said so much better by others. But, while attending an

---

110. A key abolitionist newspaper, *The Liberator* was edited by William Lloyd Garrison, the most famous of all the white abolitionists. At first, Douglass idolized him, as he tended to do with a number of people in his life, but eventually their relationship degenerated into bitter acrimony, over policy and more personal matters: in the area of policy, Douglass came to reject Garrison's belief in nonviolence as a solution to the problem of slavery. He also rejected Garrison's contention that the Constitution was a proslavery document and that the North should secede from the South. What made the break between the two so personal was Garrison's publically accusing Douglass of committing adultery with Julia Griffiths, an English abolitionist who lived with Douglass and his wife for a while in Rochester, NY. The fact of the matter is that there is no conclusive evidence that Douglass and Griffiths were lovers. Douglass also resented Garrison's disapproval of his own abolitionist paper, the *North Star*. Garrison resented his former idolizer's independence.

anti-slavery convention at Nantucket, on the 11th of August, 1841, I felt strongly moved to speak, and was at the same time much urged to do so by Mr. William C. Coffin,[111] a gentleman who had heard me speak in the colored people's meeting at New Bedford. It was a severe cross, and I took it up reluctantly. The truth was, I felt myself a slave, and the idea of speaking to white people weighed me down. I spoke but a few moments, when I felt a degree of freedom, and said what I desired with considerable ease. From that time until now, I have been engaged in pleading the cause of my brethren[112]—with what success, and with what devotion, I leave those acquainted with my labors to decide.

---

111. A banker from Nantucket.

112. It is remarkable how alike Douglass as a leader was to Madison Washington, the leader of the slave revolt on the *Creole*:

"It does not appear whether the mutineers had previously digested their plan, or not. If they had, they betrayed remarkable fidelity and efficiency in bringing it to an issue. If not, the leaders, and especially Madison Washington, manifested astonishing presence of mind and decision of character, in his movement. His reply to Merritt, when found in the hold where the women were kept—his escape to the deck, in spite of the united resistance of Merritt and Gifford—his commanding attitude and daring orders, when he stood a freeman on the slaver's deck, and his perfect preparation for the grand alternative of liberty or death, which stood before him, are splendid exemplifications of the true heroic.

"His generous leniency towards his prisoners, his oppressors—men who were carrying him and 134 others, from a condition of slavery already intolerable, to one which threatened still more galling chains, is another remarkable feature. He spared the life of the poor Frenchman, because he could not speak English, and the captain's life, at the entreaty of his wife and children. He dressed the wounds of the poor sailors who had fought against him; he spared the life of Merritt and also of young Theophilus McCargo; and when he had command of the cabin, invited the whites to partake of its refreshments. All his movements show that malice and revenge formed no part of his motives.

"Yet this leniency was accompanied with the most vigorous and efficient measures. How nobly he seems, when making Merritt pledge, at the mouth of the musket, at one o'clock at night, to navigate the vessel to New Providence; when commanding the captain and Merritt to have no communication; when placing the sailors on duty at their usual posts, and subjecting them to the same necessary restriction of non-intercourse; when pacing the deck with his three brave associates until morning, with his knife drawn, and his eye upon every spot where the least danger could arise! To heighten the moral grandeur of the scene, remember that he did not know how many of the remaining slaves might side against him; and even feared he should have to quell an insurrection against the new authority. The 19 consulted together, kept their counsels to themselves—and, so far as we can learn, exercised complete self-control over their passions, and maintained uninterrupted harmony of purpose and action." ("The Hero Mutineer," *The Liberator*, volume XII, Number 1, January 7, 1842)

As an avid reader of *The Liberator* and with a keen interest and respect for Madison Washington as the leader of a successful slave revolt, Douglass may well have had him in mind as a model for the heroic image he fashioned for himself in his 1845 *Narrative*. A key difference, though, between Madison Washington and the heroic image of Douglass is that

APPENDIX

I find, since reading over the foregoing Narrative, that I have, in several instances, spoken in such a tone and manner, respecting religion, as may possibly lead those unacquainted with my religious views to suppose me an opponent of all religion. To remove the liability of such misapprehension, I deem it proper to append the following brief explanation. What I have said respecting and against religion, I mean strictly to apply to *the slaveholding religion* of this land, and with no possible reference to Christianity proper; for, between the Christianity of this land, and the Christianity of Christ, I recognize the widest possible difference—so wide, that to receive the one as good, pure, and holy, is of necessity to reject the other as bad, corrupt, and wicked. To be the friend of the one, is of necessity to be the enemy of the other. I love the pure, peaceable, and impartial Christianity of Christ: I therefore hate the corrupt, slaveholding, women-whipping, cradle-plundering, partial and hypocritical Christianity of this land. Indeed, I can see no reason, but the most deceitful one, for calling the religion of this land Christianity. I look upon it as the climax of all misnomers, the boldest of all frauds, and the grossest of all libels. Never was there a clearer case of "stealing the livery of the court of heaven to serve the devil in."[113] I am filled with unutterable loathing when I contemplate the religious pomp and show, together with the horrible inconsistencies, which every where surround me. We have men-stealers for ministers, women-whippers for missionaries, and cradle-plunderers for church members. The man who wields the blood-clotted cowskin during the week fills the pulpit on Sunday, and claims to be a minister of the meek and lowly Jesus. The man who robs me of my earnings at the end of each week meets me as a class-leader on Sunday morning, to show me the way of life, and the path of salvation. He who sells my sister, for purposes of prostitution, stands forth as the pious advocate of purity. He who proclaims it a religious duty to read the Bible denies me the right of learning to read the name of the God who made me. He who is the religious advocate of marriage robs whole millions of its sacred influence, and leaves them to the ravages of wholesale pollution. The warm defender of the sacredness of the family relation is the same that scatters whole families,—sundering husbands and wives, parents and children, sisters and brothers,—leaving

---

the former did participate in a violent struggle for freedom, whereas Douglass did not, although he did have the opportunity but declined to join his friend John Brown in the raid on Harpers Ferry. And, although two of Douglass's sons fought for the Union in the Civil War, their father did not.

113. From Robert Pollok, *The Course of Time* (1827).

the hut vacant, and the hearth desolate. We see the thief preaching against theft, and the adulterer against adultery. We have men sold to build churches, women sold to support the gospel, and babes sold to purchase Bibles for the *Poor Heathen! All For The Glory Of God And The Good Of Souls!* The slave auctioneer's bell and the church-going bell chime in with each other, and the bitter cries of the heart-broken slave are drowned in the religious shouts of his pious master. Revivals of religion and revivals in the slave-trade go hand in hand together. The slave prison and the church stand near each other. The clanking of fetters and the rattling of chains in the prison, and the pious psalm and solemn prayer in the church, may be heard at the same time. The dealers in the bodies and souls of men erect their stand in the presence of the pulpit, and they mutually help each other. The dealer gives his blood-stained gold to support the pulpit, and the pulpit, in return, covers his infernal business with the garb of Christianity. Here we have religion and robbery the allies of each other—devils dressed in angels' robes, and hell presenting the semblance of paradise.

> "Just God! and these are they,
> Who minister at thine altar, God of right!
> Men who their hands, with prayer and blessing, lay
> On Israel's ark of light.[114]
> "What! preach, and kidnap men?
> Give thanks, and rob thy own afflicted poor?
> Talk of thy glorious liberty, and then
> Bolt hard the captive's door?
>
> "What! servants of thy own
> Merciful Son, who came to seek and save
> The homeless and the outcast, fettering down
> The tasked and plundered slave!
> "Pilate and Herod friends![115]
> Chief priests and rulers, as of old, combine!
> Just God and holy! is that church which lends
> Strength to the spoiler thine?"[116]

The Christianity of America is a Christianity, of whose votaries it may be as truly said, as it was of the ancient scribes and Pharisees, "They bind

---

114. The Holy Ark, which held the Torah.

114. The Holy Ark, which held the Torah.
115. Pilate ordered the execution of Jesus, although some question the extent of his responsibility; Herod (Antipas) gave the order for John the Baptist to be killed and was involved in the trial of Jesus.
116. From John Greenleaf Whittier, *Clerical Oppressors.*

heavy burdens, and grievous to be borne, and lay them on men's shoulders, but they themselves will not move them with one of their fingers. All their works they do for to be seen of men.—They love the uppermost rooms at feasts, and the chief seats in the synagogues, ... and to be called of men, Rabbi, Rabbi.—But woe unto you, scribes and Pharisees, hypocrites! for ye shut up the kingdom of heaven against men; for ye neither go in yourselves, neither suffer ye them that are entering to go in. Ye devour widows' houses, and for a pretence make long prayers; therefore ye shall receive the greater damnation. Ye compass sea and land to make one proselyte, and when he is made, ye make him twofold more the child of hell than yourselves.—Woe unto you, scribes and Pharisees, hypocrites! for ye pay tithe of mint, and anise, and cumin, and have omitted the weightier matters of the law, judgment, mercy, and faith; these ought ye to have done, and not to leave the other undone. Ye blind guides! which strain at a gnat, and swallow a camel. Woe unto you, scribes and Pharisees, hypocrites! for ye make clean the outside of the cup and of the platter; but within, they are full of extortion and excess.—Woe unto you, scribes and Pharisees, hypocrites! for ye are like unto whited sepulchres, which indeed appear beautiful outward, but are within full of dead men's bones, and of all uncleanness. Even so ye also outwardly appear righteous unto men, but within ye are full of hypocrisy and iniquity."

Dark and terrible as is this picture, I hold it to be strictly true of the overwhelming mass of professed Christians in America. They strain at a gnat, and swallow a camel. Could any thing be more true of our churches? They would be shocked at the proposition of fellowshipping a *sheep-stealer*; and at the same time they hug to their communion a man-stealer, and brand me with being an infidel, if I find fault with them for it. They attend with Pharisaical strictness to the outward forms of religion, and at the same time neglect the weightier matters of the law, judgment, mercy, and faith. They are always ready to sacrifice, but seldom to show mercy. They are they who are represented as professing to love God whom they have not seen, whilst they hate their brother whom they have seen. They love the heathen on the other side of the globe. They can pray for him, pay money to have the Bible put into his hand, and missionaries to instruct him; while they despise and totally neglect the heathen at their own doors.

Such is, very briefly, my view of the religion of this land; and to avoid any misunderstanding, growing out of the use of general terms, I mean by the religion of this land, that which is revealed in the words, deeds, and actions, of those bodies, north and south, calling themselves Christian churches, and yet in union with slaveholders. It is against religion, as presented by these bodies, that I have felt it my duty to testify.

I conclude these remarks by copying the following portrait of the religion of the south, (which is, by communion and fellowship, the religion of the north,) which I soberly affirm is "true to the life," and without caricature or the slightest exaggeration. It is said to have been drawn, several years before the present anti-slavery agitation began, by a northern Methodist preacher, who, while residing at the south, had an opportunity to see slave-holding morals, manners, and piety, with his own eyes. "Shall I not visit for these things? saith the Lord. Shall not my soul be avenged on such a nation as this?"[117]

A PARODY[118]
"Come, saints and sinners, hear me tell
How pious priests whip Jack and Nell,
And women buy and children sell,
And preach all sinners down to hell,
And sing of heavenly union.
"They'll bleat and baa, dona like goats,
Gorge down black sheep, and strain at motes,
Array their backs in fine black coats,
Then seize their negroes by their throats,
And choke, for heavenly union.
"They'll church you if you sip a dram,
And damn you if you steal a lamb;
Yet rob old Tony, Doll, and Sam,
Of human rights, and bread and ham;
Kidnapper's heavenly union.
"They'll loudly talk of Christ's reward,
And bind his image with a cord,
And scold, and swing the lash abhorred,
And sell their brother in the Lord
To handcuffed heavenly union.
"They'll read and sing a sacred song,
And make a prayer both loud and long,
And teach the right and do the wrong,
Hailing the brother, sister throng,
With words of heavenly union.
"We wonder how such saints can sing,
Or praise the Lord upon the wing,
Who roar, and scold, and whip, and sting,

---

117. Jeremiah 5:9.
118. This is a parody of a popular hymn, "Heavenly Union," which was often sung in white churches in the South in the nineteenth century.

And to their slaves and mammon cling,
In guilty conscience union.
"They'll raise tobacco, corn, and rye,
And drive, and thieve, and cheat, and lie,
And lay up treasures in the sky,
By making switch and cowskin fly,
In hope of heavenly union.
"They'll crack old Tony on the skull,
And preach and roar like Bashan bull,
Or braying ass, of mischief full,
Then seize old Jacob by the wool,
And pull for heavenly union.
"A roaring, ranting, sleek man-thief,
Who lived on mutton, veal, and beef,
Yet never would afford relief
To needy, sable sons of grief,
Was big with heavenly union.
"'Love not the world,' the preacher said,
And winked his eye, and shook his head;
He seized on Tom, and Dick, and Ned,
Cut short their meat, and clothes, and bread,
Yet still loved heavenly union.
"Another preacher whining spoke
Of One whose heart for sinners broke:
He tied old Nanny to an oak,
And drew the blood at every stroke,
And prayed for heavenly union.
"Two others oped their iron jaws,
And waved their children-stealing paws;
There sat their children in gewgaws;
By stinting negroes' backs and maws,
They kept up heavenly union.

"All good from Jack another takes,
And entertains their flirts and rakes,
Who dress as sleek as glossy snakes,
And cram their mouths with sweetened cakes;
And this goes down for union."

Sincerely and earnestly hoping that this little book may do something toward throwing light on the American slave system, and hastening the glad day of deliverance to the millions of my brethren in bonds—faithfully relying upon the power of truth, love, and justice, for success in my humble efforts—and solemnly pledging my self anew to the sacred cause,— I subscribe myself,

> FREDERICK DOUGLASS.
> LYNN, *Mass., April* 28, 1845.[119]
> THE END

---

119. Just four years later in 1849, in a speech to the American Colonization Society, Douglass said he would welcome the news that the slaves had distributed "death and devastation" throughout the South; this is far from his earlier support for Garrison's idea that slavery should be abolished peacefully. Douglass changed his positions on many controversies throughout his lifetime, which some have criticized, while others have praised his shifting stances as intellectual flexibility. He consistently opposed colonization, the return of African Americans to Africa, however.

Bibliography

Andrews, William L. *To Tell a Free Story: The First Century of Afro-American Autobiography, 1760–1865*. Urbana and Chicago: University of Illinois Press, 1986.

Blight, David W. *Race and Reunion: The Civil War in American Memory*. Cambridge, MA: Belknap Press of Harvard University Press, 2001.

Blight, David W. *Frederick Douglass' Civil War: Keeping Faith in Jubilee*. Baton Rouge: Louisiana State University Press, 1989.

Bruce, Dickson D., Jr. *The Origins of African American Literature, 1680–1865*. Charlottesville: University of Virginia Press, 2001.

Butterfield, Stephen. *Black Autobiography in America*. Amherst: University of Massachusetts Press, 1974.

Cartwright, Keith. *Reading Africa into American Literature*. Lexington: The University Press of Kentucky, 2002.

Diedrich, Maria. *Love Across the Color Lines: Ottilie Assing and Frederick Douglass*. New York: Hill and Wang, 1999.

Douglass, Frederick. 1979. *Frederick Douglass Papers*. Edited by John W. Blassingame. New Haven, CT: Yale University Press, 1979.

Douglass, Frederick. *The Heroic Slave*. Edited by Robert S. Levine, John Stauffer, and John R. McKivigan. New Haven, CT: Yale University Press, 2013.

Felgar, Robert. *American Slavery: A Historical Exploration of Literature*. Santa Barbara, CA: Greenwood Press, 2015.

Felgar, Robert. "The Rediscovery of Frederick Douglass." *Mississippi Quarterly* 35 (1982): 427–438.

Huggins, Nathan Irvin. *Slave and Citizen: The Life of Frederick Douglass*. Boston, MA: Little, Brown and Company, 1980.

Levine, Robert S. *The Lives of Frederick Douglass*. Cambridge, MA: Harvard University Press, 2016.

Levine, Robert S., and Samuel Otter, eds. *Frederick Douglass & Herman Melville: Essays in Relation*. Chapel Hill: The University of North Carolina Press, 2008.

McFeeley, William S. *Frederick Douglass*. New York: W.W. Norton & Company, 1991.

Martin, Waldo E., Jr. *The Mind of Frederick Douglass*. Chapel Hill: University of North Carolina Press, 1984.

Muller, John. *Frederick Douglass in Washington, D.C.: The Lion of Anacostia.* Charleston, SC: The History Press, 2012.

Preston, Dickson J. *Young Frederick Douglass: The Maryland Years.* Baltimore and London: Johns Hopkins University Press, 1980.

Stauffer, John. *The Black Hearts of Men: Radical Abolitionists and the Transformation of Race.* Cambridge, MA: Harvard University Press, 2002.

Sundquist, Eric. *To Wake the Nations: Race in the Making of American Literature.* Cambridge, MA: Belknap Press of Harvard University Press, 1993.

Wallace, Maurice D. *Constructing the Black Masculine: Identity and Ideality in African American Men's Literature and Culture, 1795–1995.* Dunham, NC: Duke University Press Books, 2002.

Wells, Ida B., Frederick Douglass, Irvine Garland Penn, and Ferdinand L. Barnett. *The Reason Why the Colored American Is Not in the World's Columbian Exposition: The Afro-American's Contribution to Columbian Literature.* Edited by Robert W. Rydell. Urbana and Chicago: University of Illinois Press, 1999.

Wilson, William J. "A Leaf from My Scrapbook: Samuel R. Ward and Frederick Douglass." In *Douglass in His Own Time.* Edited by John Ernest. Iowa City: University of Iowa Press, 2014. Originally published in Julia Griffiths, ed., *Autographs for Freedom.* Auburn, NY: Alden, Beardsley, 1854, 165–173.

ଓଃଡ଼ୋ

Index

About the Author

Robert Felgar, PhD, is professor of English and department head at Jacksonville State University, Jacksonville, Alabama. His published works include *American Slavery: A Historical Exploration of Literature*, *Understanding Richard Wright's Black Boy: A Student Casebook to Issues, Sources, and Historical Documents*, and *Student Companion to Richard Wright*. Felgar holds a doctorate in English from Duke University.